301

A History of Grassington

CW01622058

£1.25

A History of Grassington

by

Susan D. Brooks

DALESMAN BOOKS
1979

THE DALESMAN PUBLISHING COMPANY LTD., CLAPHAM (via Lancaster), NORTH YORKSHIRE

First published 1979

© Susan D. Brooks 1979

ISBN: 0 85206 516 7

Printed in Great Britain by
GEORGE TODD & SON
Marlborough Street, Whitehaven

Contents

The cover photographs show: Front—Grassington Square in the mid-19th century, with the Liverpool Warehouse (left) and the cottage now housing the Museum (centre) (Upper Wharfedale Museum Society). Back, top: Strip lynchets near Grassington (author). Back, bottom: Grass Wood and Cove Closes (R. W. Cooper).

Preface

SEVERAL small books have been written about Grassington; mainly to help visitors to explore it and its surroundings. This is the first to attempt an account of its history making use of original documents and other sources, many of them not available to the early writers. If these show some of the well known traditions and theories to have been fanciful, it is hoped that the extra information will compensate for this.

I have used extensively the Skipton Castle papers and Calendars of State Papers at the Yorkshire Archaeological Society, the Borthwick Institute, York, and Skipton and other libraries. Much other material has been collected over many years from individuals who have kindly lent me deeds and other papers, far too many to acknowledge or indeed to use. I am most grateful. But behind all this has been the background and foundation laid by Dr. Raistrick's W.E.A. lectures which whetted my appetite. Last but not least I owe a very great deal to the late Mrs. Waters (Rose Birch to her contemporaries), who in my early years at Grassington took me into the byways and corners of the township, sharing with me her very wide knowledge of names and places and her feeling for history. I have missed her very much while writing this book.

My thanks are also due to those who have provided me with extra illustrative material.

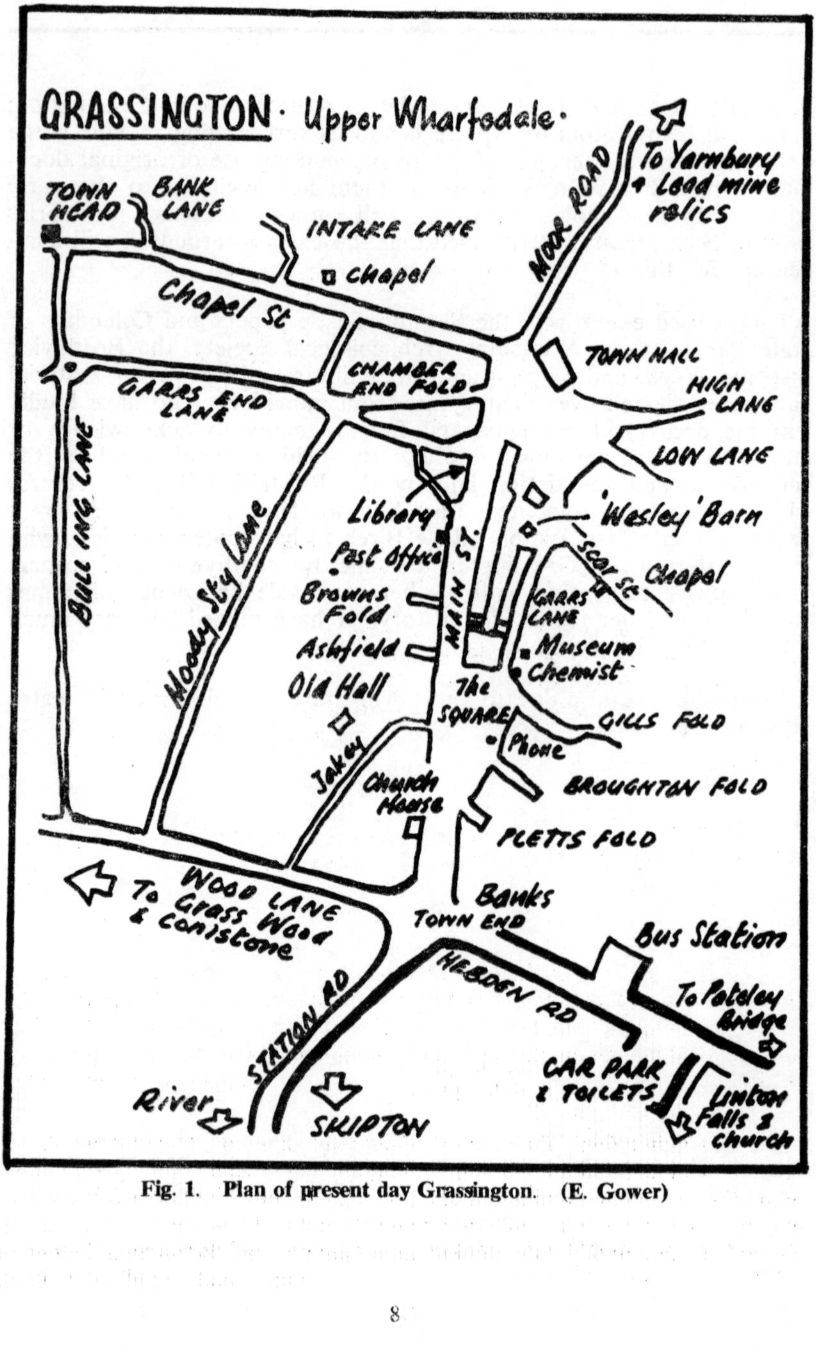

Fig. 1. Plan of present day Grassington. (E. Gower)

Introduction

NINE HUNDRED years ago Grassington was already a well established village with at least 300 acres of arable land and meadow on which tax was paid to the king. Domesday Book recorded this in the year 1087. The village must therefore have been founded several generations previously, probably sometime early in the 7th century. We have no written documents about it in those early days, but we can build up a general idea of what the land was like and how the village began and grew, from writings about similar communities elsewhere. But we must remember that the physical features of Upper Wharfedale would have an influence which would affect the community from the very beginning.

Pre-History

Long before the present Grassington began there had been settlements of Celtic Ancient Britons mainly in Grass Wood and on the higher land above it and between it and the village. All this is a well-drained limestone area where the original forest would be thinner than on the wetter soils stretching to the Hebden boundary. The footpath from Town Head towards Conistone passes through some of the best signs of this pre-historic Iron Age occupation, which lasted from somewhere about 500 BC to the end of the Roman rule in England.

It is difficult to imagine the whole dale except the present moorland covered with trees, thick forest merging into more open woodland and thin scrub in the higher parts. The Celtic people with their primitive tools chose the limestone area because of its smaller trees, ashes rather than oaks. Probably the thickest forest of all was on the slopes on a level with and below the village. Here a large glacial moraine had been left by the last great valley glacier of the Ice Age, and though the forest grew thickly it was the acorns and other fruits and roots and animal life which would be of more value than the timber to these people.

As the centuries passed the greater part of the forest was gradually cleared, but the small fields of these early cultivators had evidently reverted to woodland and never been cleared again, since an indenture of sale in the mid-18th century mentions the right of certain people to take hazel wood for fencing from that area. There was still much more woodland than today.

We can only surmise as to what caused the Celts to abandon their Grassington, and other, settlements. The theory was put forward that when the Romans left there were great empty villas and farmlands into which the British gradually moved from less productive areas. Recent research into life in the Roman settlements has made it clear that the Romans who went away from some of these colonies were only a small proportion of the population and that the British workers and their families had adopted the Roman way of life and carried on the settlements. Whether the Grassington settlers moved east to the plains or not is unknown. Life there would be very different for them if they did.

What does seem clear without doubt is that the next wave of settlers found the area almost if not quite unpopulated but they did not take over the deserted settlements.

The Coming of the Angles

IN the later years of the Roman occupation of Britain the East Coast was repeatedly raided by Angles from what is now the coast of Germany, while the Saxons raided further south. After the Romans left Britain, about 450 AD, the raiders began to stay and settle, both on the coast and inland. They soon overpowered the native Celtic Britons and, in the next two centuries, developed from raiders into a civilized people in a large kingdom called Northumbria. They had become Christians and had two great centres of learning at Lindisfarne and Durham. But to the east of Wharfedale the way inland was blocked by strong resistance from the small remaining British kingdom of Elmete just beyond Leeds, which was not overcome till 616. After that the Angles began to move into the Dales and many new settlements were made among which were Grassington and its neighbours, Hebden and Conistone. Their story, had they written it, would have read in many ways like that of the American pioneers moving west from the coastal settlements of the Pilgrim Fathers. In spite of the lapse of time between, the two had much in common.

Pioneer settlers, wherever they may be, have three basic needs, water, fuel and shelter. Our group of Angles looking for a way down into the valley, would easily notice the thinner woods of the limestone, and if they saw the remains of the earlier settlers' huts and fields, they would be likely to avoid them. It is quite possible that if they had nominally accepted Christianity they still held many of their old superstitions. What probably guided them was one of the very few streams in the limestone area, which they followed down until it led to a reasonably level stretch on which they could make their first 'ton', the beginnings of the village. The stream is still there, though hidden in a culvert right down the village. The first wooden huts made from nearby trees surrounded a space which later, and until not so long ago, was the Market Place, now the Square.

An important essential also for new settlers was land suitable for crops, and this they must have won bit by bit as they cleared the trees from the moraine covered slopes below the village and further afield. This was very difficult to plough, not only because of the slope but because of the great numbers of stones and boulders, though the soil was fertile. Many boulders and stones had to be moved and were collected in long lines along the slope about eleven yards apart, and then the land in between the rows ploughed. Because of the slope all the furrows had to be ploughed the same way, with the sods turned downhill, and this gradually moved the soil down towards the lower row of stones, building up a series of steps separated by steep "risers." These terraces are known locally as raines, but the textbooks call them strip lynchets, and they are a very noticeable feature of the Dales landscape, though in Grassington very much disguised by walls and recent housing. The illustration (back cover—top) shows a 'flight' of lynchets on the way to Burnsall, which is very easy to see. One way to discover one of Grassington's best series is to take the footpath from the Wharfe bridge straight up which continues across and along roads among houses to the top of the village, but still shows the terraced formation.

In this way the young Anglian community began to tame and mould the landscape. We cannot follow it step by step. It is not until after the Norman Conquest that we have the first documentary evidence of the community in the Domesday Book, under the name Ghersintone, and with much of the eventual arable area already cultivated.

Before that there had been two more invasions of Upper Wharfedale but of much less importance and neither seriously affected Grassington. The first was that of the Danes, which led to the conquest of much of England and the rule of King Canute. It came no nearer Grassington than Thorpe in Burnsall parish, founded after a treaty in the year 876. Early in the next century a very different incursion occurred, this time by Norsemen or Vikings, an overflow from a Norse settlement in Ireland. These people landed on the West Coast and came inland, chiefly settling on the high open uplands as scattered sheep farmers, so far as the Dales were concerned. They did for a short period send one stream towards York where they set up a Viking kingdom but that did not affect Wharfedale. The peaceful sheep farmers of Kilnsey and other moorland expanses became important later, but only one isolated settlement within Grassington's boundaries may have originated in this way, namely Botton on the Conistone-Grassington boundary. These family farms never developed into large villages.

These three strains of North European origin were not racially very different and their languages had much in common. The result was that the English, which in the end developed in Upper Wharfedale, was a dialect in which Danish and Norse words played a large part, and, in spite of Radio and T.V., a conversation between farmers at, say, Kilnsey Show, can completely puzzle visitors from the southern counties even now.

The Norman Conquest and After

WHEN William of Normandy became king of England in 1066 he took over a country well organised on the whole in local government. His predecessor, Edward the Confessor, had ruled over an England divided into shires, which in turn were divided into hundreds or wapentakes as they were called in Yorkshire and other parts formerly under Danish rule. Grassington was in the wapentake of Staincliffe until the changes in 1973 when the name was quietly dropped. Both shire and wapentake had their own courts under the Shire-reeve, later the Sheriff. William kept both these in force, only later introducing his own judges and courts with over-riding powers.

At township level William also found as a rule a satisfactory system of law and order. Most villages had a thegn (or thane) who was a lesser nobleman, responsible to an overlord or directly to the king. Under him was the folk-moot, the remote ancestor of the parish council, and various officials. Of these the most important was the reeve, who was responsible for organising and supervising the seasonal work on the land, the crops, the pastures and the workers' tasks. The only change William made in most cases was to replace the thegn by a Norman Lord of the Manor, though the actual choice was not usually his. He parcelled out all the country apart from royal estates among the comparatively few Norman barons who had helped him to win the kingdom, and gave them the right to grant out much smaller, and usually scattered, estates to their friends and relations. The units of these estates were called manors, which were often exactly the same as the English townships in area, but a manor was much more than a township. Initially the only change this made to Grassington was that Gamelbar, the thegn who according to Domesday Book "had" Ghersintone in the time of King Edward, disappeared. That was before 1087. The first Lord of the Manor, after an initial confusion, was Nigel de Plumpton who by 1190 held the manor from the great family of Percy, who in turn held it from the king with a large number of others. We have to speak of the king "granting" and the barons and others "holding" because for several centuries after this the king claimed all land as his own, which he could, and did, reclaim if the holder in any way offended. This actually did happen in the case of Linton and Threshfield but never in Grassington.

The Manor of Grassington and its Lords

To understand much in the history of Grassington, or any other village, it is necessary to know just what is implied by the manor. Though on a map it looks exactly the same as the township, it is very much more.

To the king a manor was the smallest unit of local government and he relied on the Lord to keep it in order. To the Lord of the Manor it was a source of income and his prestige was largely measured by the number and condition of those he held. There was not as a rule much personal contact between the Lord and his manors; often they were far too widely spaced. His bailiffs or stewards acted on his behalf and much depended on their character.

In each manor the Lord reserved for himself some of the best arable and pasture land, and, in Grassington, Grass Wood also. All this was called the demesne. The villeins, as the ordinary people were called, held strips of arable land scattered in the open fields and had pasture rights on the common pasture and, in Grassington, turbary rights for peat from the Moor instead of wood. In return for this the villeins had to give a stated number of days work on the demesne or as craftsmen, etc., according to their skills. By the 15th century, though still tied to work for the Lord, they had begun to pay rent and receive wages. Much of this money went back to the Lord, besides the rent, in dues payable after a death, or a change of tenancy, for permission to marry outside the manor, or to go away for education; in fact almost anything outside the ordinary course of life. The Lord's Manor Court dealt with all affairs relating to law and order and the custom of the manor, though as time went on the churchwardens acted in cases of sin as distinct from crime.

Another source of profit for the Lord in some manors, including Grassington, was a market and a fair. A Latin charter of 1282 translated reads:

> York. Robert de Plumpton gave the King ten pounds for the institution of a market on his Manor of Grassington and a fair in the same.

The charter continued with details of days and dates. The market was to be held each Friday and the fair at Michaelmas. Fairs were usually held on or about the feast-day of the patron saint of the parish church and the fair here was therefore to be on the day before and the day after September 29th, the Feast of St. Michael and All Angels. Linton Parish included Linton, Threshfield and Hebden as well as Grassington so this fair could not be held as was usual near the parish church which was in Linton manor. As far as we know people from the other villages were allowed to come to Grassington as they had no fair or market of their own (see front cover photograph).

On both market and fair days there were officials on the look out for sharp practices of any kind and fines were imposed on the spot, and these also went to swell the total of £30 12s 4d which was the estimated value of Grassington to the Plumpton of the day in Henry VII's reign; equal to several thousand pounds today.

In the case of Grassington and most other small manors the Lord only paid occasional visits to his Manor House or Hall. These visits had at least three purposes. First, they were made to inspect the manor as a whole, and there are signs at a later date that this was not done very thoroughly at Grassington. Secondly, a lot of the produce of the demesne would be consumed on the spot, meat, meal or flour, and so avoid transport elsewhere. Fodder for the horses and draught oxen would be needed as well as food for the Lord's family and servants, and of course the eggs in which some of the manor dues would be paid, whether at Easter or not. The third purpose is not often mentioned but was important in another way and was a matter of 'spring cleaning'. In the days before modern hygiene and sanitation, big houses with a large central hall in which many people ate, slept and spent much of their time, and where dogs roamed freely over the rush-strewn floor, became indescribably filthy and noisome, and even the far from fastidious owner found it necessary to go away so that the hall and its surroundings could be thoroughly cleaned. How often that happened depended upon circumstances, but the Plumptons had several not very distant manors from Spofforth, their main home. One of these was Nesfield near Bolton Abbey.

Grassington Old Hall, as it is known today, was never large and has been restored and added to so many times that it has no definite style of architecture, some small parts being according to Pevsner 14th century, but much 17th century and even later. It probably stands on the site of the first Anglian head man's wooden hut, erected when the village was first settled, and for that no date can be given.

Who then, if anyone, did live regularly at the Hall in the early times? There is one possible occupier named before 1600; that was John de Scardeburgh in 1379. A letter written by Robert de Plumpton to the tenant of another manorial hall suggests a similar case. This man paid a moderate rent for the hall and demesne of the rented manor, but had to make all arrangements when Robert announced his impending arrival. An extensive list of what was expected was given, accommodation and supplies with all the tenant's duties. It is quite possible that John de Scardeburgh was a similar tenant of Grassington Hall and demesne. Reasons for thinking this will emerge later. It is possible that evidence of much more contact between the Plumptons and Grassington will be discovered in some documents unearthed in recent years.

How the Plumptons came to have Grassington is a bit vague as the first mention is the marriage of one of them to a widow, Isabella Westwick, Lady of Grassington, about 1190, with no details at all. About that time, (dates are far from exactly given in those days), Nigel de Plumpton signed a grant to the Abbot of Fountains and in 1319 another Nigel signed a charter to another abbot at Grassington. These and one other similar superscription to a charter are all the evidence we have of the Plumptons and Grassington for many generations. The family was involved in the Wars of the Roses, the senior member being killed at the Battle of Towton. His son Robert then gave the manor to his widowed mother. After that there is again silence until the late 16th century. Then Sir Ingram Clifford had acquired Grassington by marriage with a Plumpton heiress and, having no son, disposed of it to George Clifford, 3rd Earl of Cumberland of Skipton Castle, partly by sale and the remainder by will. In that way Grassington in 1597 came wholly into the Clifford estates, with the Earl as Lord of the Manor, but much happened before then.

The Township and the People

THOUGH the manor played a very large part in the life of the village and its people, there were other facets in which the Lord and his officials had no control. In the centuries before Henry VIII did so much to upset the old order, there were a number of events or other matters which, though not of great historic importance, must have in some degree influenced the character of the people and therefore of the village.

The Scots' Raids

Foraging parties of Scots were likely to appear in the North of England at any time for centuries and in many areas. In the years just before and after 1318 a series of very bad raids, amounting almost to war, caused great havoc as the Scots moved southwards east of the Pennines, Fountains Abbey being particularly badly damaged. Then they moved westward, pillaging Bolton Priory and turned north up the Dales. Most of the damage was done by the Scots of course, but the English forces trying to drive them back north were not blameless, living off the land through which they passed. The Abbot of Fountains wrote to the Superior of the Cistercian Order asking for help on account of the havoc caused in this way in the Abbey's lands in Upper Wharfedale, especially Kilnsey and thereabouts.

There are no records of damage done to separate villages, but some idea is given by figures relating to whole parishes. In 1292 Pope Nicholas, at the request of King Henry III, caused a valuation to be made of all the parishes in England. This would refer only to the parish church and all its possessions and endowments. Linton parish was then assessed at £33 6s 8d. Then in 1318 the king ordered another valuation which was given as £26 13s 4d, so the decrease was only £6 13s 4d or 20 marks. For comparison that amount was exactly that of the stipend of Brother John, vicar at Kirkby Malham, about that time. From this it is clear that the damage was comparatively slight in material terms, but, as we know today, that is not all and some Grassington people at least may have been sorely troubled.

Grassington and the Monks

Fountains Abbey had, from soon after its founding, a large estate at Kilnsey and on the moors to the west, but no land at all in Grassington township except for a small area, the gift of which was not confirmed, between Grass Wood and the boundary. But as long as the abbey existed, that is till 1539, there was considerable movement of men and animals, pack ponies and ox-waggons, between Kilnsey with its large production of wool, and the Abbey near Ripon. Therefore, it has been said, monks must frequently have been seen passing through Grassington. This however is wrong on two accounts. First there is the widespread use of the word 'monk' to refer to anyone from, or connected with, the Abbey, whereas most of the men travelling were either lay-brothers or paid employees. Monks were comparatively few in number, only 33 at Fountains at the Dissolution in 1539, and they were fully committed to the religious life, the original purpose of all monasteries. Only special officials among them, e.g., the Cellarer and the Bursar, travelled on Abbey business and it is to these that we owe the Abbey records of accounts and rents.

The earliest of the very few records of contracts of any kind between Grassington and Kilnsey grange, the Abbey headquarters, is a very early one. About 1190 Nigel de Plumpton gave the Abbot and the community right of passage through his lands of Grassington avoiding corn and meadow. This meant that everything had to keep above the village in the open common pasture, and in so doing they would mark out a roadway roughly that of the old highway from Grassington to Hebden (High Lane). The journey to and from Kilnsey was too long for unnecessary diversions into villages, the second reason for seeing so little of the Abbey people, monks or otherwise, in the village.

Two entries in the Abbey records tell us a little more and give us actual names. About 1400 William Cookson was paid for the delivery of a load of lead from Grassington. A few years later Robert Holme of Grassington made a will from which the Bursar quotes, 'Seeing that great danger from pestilence among his family and descendants which has struck his house and killed two of his off-spring he has made his will and has bequeathed to the Abbot and Convent of Fountains 40 shillings worth of lead for his absolution', that is for masses for his soul.

The lead mentioned was almost certainly from the very early lines of opencast workings still clearly visible from the Grassington-Conistone footpath across Lea Green, which are on or very near the route which Nigel de Plumpton had in mind, so the handing over of the lead would be a simple matter. But whose lead was it? Did the Plumpton of that time know about it? It was from his land.

The Black Death

The pestilence mentioned by Robert Holme was not the Black Death, which happened over a hundred years earlier. Epidemics were no uncommon occurrence and the one mentioned may possibly have been more disastrous locally than the Black Death in 1349. We have slight evidence that that great plague was less severe in Craven than some other places in Yorkshire. In a list of York Diocese deaneries, giving the percentage of clergy who died in the various deaneries. Craven's figure was only 27%, that is including Wharfedale, while York, Ainsty and Pontefract had 37-42%. In rural Grassington the percentage was probably lower than 27%.

The 1379 Poll Tax

In the Middle Ages no complete census was ever taken and it is difficult to get even an approximate number. In 1379 the Parliament allowed the king to levy a Poll Tax on all males and single women between the ages of 16 and 60. Married women, clergy, paupers and idiots were exempt. The resulting lists can be used as a rough guide to population numbers. It is usual to allow three children to each married couple and to neglect the very few who would be over 60. In this way the number for Grassington works out as 137.

The tax paid was a basic 4 pence, i.e. a groat, but there were higher rates for craftsmen and others. In Grassington two tailors each paid 6 pence, a tanner paid a shilling and one man John de Scardeburgh was assessed at 3 shillings and 4 pence. He must have been a well-to-do freeholder and, as was suggested in an earlier chapter, he must have been the tenant of the Hall. His surname signifies where he or his family came from and there were others similarly named. Others had occupation names, Smith, Shepherd, etc. Choosing a surname, which many of them had not had to do before, was not always easy. Some "son" names were included and one Sneksdoghter was obviously a woman. One man chose, or perhaps had chosen for him, the possibly descriptive name of Gauke, but another man was accepted with only one name, Marmaduke, very unusual and therefore not likely to be duplicated.

The Troublous 1500s

THE long drawn out Wars of the Roses between the Dukes of Lancaster and York ended at the Battle of Bosworth in 1485, without Grassington having had any known involvement. In the next century conflict of different origins came much nearer. First there was the periodically renewed threat of invasion by the Scots, culminating in the Battle of Flodden in 1513. A few years before this Henry Clifford, the Shepherd Lord of popular legend, planned to lead a force from his followers to join the king's troops. He mustered his men and among them four from Grassington. As there had recently been a marriage between his family and that of the Plumptons, Grassington's Lord must have agreed to this. Their names were John Clarke, John Wilkinson, George Knolle and Leonard Hibbertson. Their leader was John Clarke who had his own bow and a fully equipped horse, and was described as 'able', which seems to have meant trained. The other three each had a bow but nothing else, unless arrows were taken for granted. A far cry this from the knights in shining armour riding out to war on their prancing steeds from the Hall, as imagined by Bailey Harker, a Grassington born author, in 1869. There is no record as to whether these men actually fought at Flodden, but some time later a Kilnsey man bequeathed his sword in his will, 'if it come back from Scotland'.

Henry VIII and his Works

The rest of the 16th century was a time of great changes in social, political and religious affairs involved in the policy of King Henry VIII and his successors, Edward VI, Mary and Elizabeth. From what we know of Grassington at the time, it escaped the more violent conflicts arising but nevertheless it must have been a period of uncertainty and sometimes fear.

Henry had come to the throne in 1509 and soon put forward laws aimed at keeping the lower classes of society strictly in their respective places by rules about dress and even food. He was alarmed at the general improvement in conditions which was slowly but steadily occurring. He then turned to reformation of the Church and in 1536, with his Chancellor, Cardinal Wolsey, and with the Pope's consent, he closed a number of poverty stricken and, in some cases, corrupt monasteries and convents. Wolsey intended to devote their funds to educational purposes but did not get very far. The result of all this was a flood of rumours, grossly exaggerated, as to what the king would do next.

At the same time there was growing trouble in the country between landlords and tenants where landlords were enclosing land for their own use, robbing tenants of their rights. There were riots against the Cliffords of Skipton Castle in the Giggleswick area, but again Grassington seems to have escaped. There is one large 40 acre field today, High Close, which may have been enclosed about this time but is more likely to have been much earlier when the Plumptons were more active. It was part of the Lord's demesne but its enclosure left the tenants with adequate pasture.

Pilgrimage of Grace

It is not to be wondered at that, in an age when there was no printed news or radio, rumours got out of hand and tempers rose so that eventually resistance became rife. In 1536 a rising began in Lincolnshire and spread into Yorkshire and through the northern Dales towards Lancashire.

It was a rising of 'the commons', that is those below the rank of gentry, but a number of gentry joined them of their own accord and others were coerced. The leaders emphasised the religious aims of the protest by hoisting a banner bearing five crosses representing the five wounds of Christ in Roman Catholic symbolism. The rank and file were much more concerned with their relations with the landlords. They tried without success to get the Cliffords to join them, so Skipton Castle was besieged. In view of what happened later it is worth noting that the Nortons, Lords of Rylstone and Threshfield, joined the siege; they were never friendly towards the Cliffords.

The course of the rising, known as the Pilgrimage of Grace, is most confused. In the end several thousand almost entirely unarmed 'troops' marched towards London, were met by king's officers at Pontefract, promised pardon and consideration of their grievances if they would return home quietly. They did return and that was the end of a futile gesture for most of them. There is no record of any Grassington men being among them. The Plumptons were not involved. But unrest was still simmering in some places. Some months later there was an outbreak of rioting among Clifford tenants beyond Gargrave which produced confused results in which Grassington became slightly involved. It was decided that notices should be posted on the doors of the churches of Gargrave, Rylstone and Linton telling parishioners 'to be at Rylstone on Tuesday next at 9 o'clock to kill any deer you may find'. Why Rylstone when the Nortons had been against the Cliffords in the rising? Rylstone Park was kept for Norton deer. It is possible that this notice was a code message giving time and place for a meeting not concerned with deer at all, but part of a larger planned rising. However, Clifford supporters from Skipton prevented this raid, but exactly what happened is not known. It would be interesting to know how Grassington people got on with those from Threshfield and Linton the following Sunday at church! One imagines that feelings continued to simmer in all parts of the dale, but in spite of Henry's breach with Rome and the growth of Protestantism under King Edward VI and Elizabeth, and the very short reign of the Roman Catholic Queen Mary, there is little known about Grassington's attitude throughout. No Linton rectors got into trouble.

Henry's big attack on the Church in 1539 in closing all the remaining monasteries affected Grassington very little, since it had no monastic holdings in the township. One small area beyond Grass Wood had belonged to Fountains Abbey for only a short time. Probably more upsetting to the village was a very different matter in 1539, when Henry ordered a muster of men fit to join his forces against the Scots. This muster was to be held throughout Craven. This, unlike the Flodden roll, was in no way connected with the manor. The constable of the village, who was responsible to the Justices of the Peace, had the duty of seeing the roll made and of selecting from it the number of men actually required by the king's officials. The roll which still exists contains the names of 31 men between the ages of 16 and 60. The summary at the end, somewhat simplified, reads as follows:

Sum of able men		31	
wherof —	Archers	11	
	Billmen	20	
Thereof —	of furnished	5	(i.e. with horse, equipped)
	of horse	4	
	of iakke	8	(jack, a leather jerkin)
	of salette	4	(metal helmet)
	of bil	4	(a weapon)

Again we do not know how many, if any, of these men actually served with the king.

During the next 30 years Henry died, and his son Edward VI's reign saw a drastic removal from the churches of everything connected with the Mass, and the introduction of the Protestant Book of Common Prayer. Edward only reigned for five years and then Queen Mary, a fanatical Roman Catholic, followed and immediately brought back the Mass and burnt large numbers of Protestants at the stake. She also only reigned five years and then Elizabeth became queen and tried to bring about a middle way between the extremes of her two predecessors. Clergy and laity alike were in confusion. The heretics of one reign became the faithful of the next and one wonders if, in churches remote from ecclesiastical authority, the changes were fully carried out. The only local person who suffered for his faith in this period, as far as is known, was William Dean, born in Grassington about 1530. He went to school in Leeds, then to Magdalen College, Oxford. He was ordained and served as a Protestant vicar, but then came under Roman Catholic influence and fled, like many others, to Douai in France. There he became a Roman Catholic priest and was sent on secret missions to England. On one of these he was caught and hanged, not it was said for his beliefs, but because he had committed treason by disobeying Elizabeth's injunctions. This was in 1588 and did not in any way involve Grassington people, unless he still had relatives living there.

Rising of the North

Earlier in Elizabeth's reign than this, in 1569, another rebellion broke out, much more serious than the Pilgrimage of Grace, among the northern aristocracy who were ardent Catholics. Led by the Earls of Westmorland and Northumberland they carried many of their tenants with them and Richard Norton had followers from Threshfield and Linton village. The Cliffords were always loyal to the crown and maybe their influence kept Grassington men out of the conflict, though the manor was not yet theirs.

The rebels this time had good leadership and Mary Queen of Scots, whom all Catholics hoped would replace Elizabeth as queen, was for a time held prisoner at Bolton Castle in Wensleydale, so strengthening the Catholic morale. This time the crown sent an armed force and the rising was crushed. The two Earls fled abroad, Richard Norton lost his lands and was executed with many others. The queen sent drastic orders. Several men were to be hanged in every village from which rebels had come, 'for terror'. Linton and Threshfield had two each and others were from Rylstone and Malhamdale, with another local man to act as hangman. There is no mention of anyone from Grassington in these lists or in a long list of over 2000 pardoned, only one of which was from Upper Wharfedale, a Kilnsey man.

After this the 16th century came to an end without any more wars and rebellions. Grassington's ordinary life had carried on through the peaceful and not so peaceful times. From now on we have good documentary evidence of how the whole township had been brought into use, and this we owe to George, Earl of Cumberland, who had recently become Lord of the Manor.

George, 3rd Earl of Cumberland

GEORGE Clifford, the 3rd Earl, was one of the most colourful of his family, but was little known in Skipton. As soon as he inherited the Lordship, in 1597, he made it clear that he was hoping to rebuild his family fortune. This he had lost in unsuccessful voyages against Spanish galleons on the high seas. Several times he was fitted out with ships by the queen or at his own expense, but nearly always he failed. Yet Elizabeth thought highly of him as her letters show.

His first step was to arrange mortgages with most of the tenants whereby they received a lease of their holdings for a short term in return for a lump sum repayable at a fixed date. This is rather an unusual form of mortgage and Whitaker in 'The History of Craven' states that the Earl mortgaged the manor to his tenants. This is not so. Individual leases show that the Lord's manorial rights were carefully reserved. Only the tenants' lands and buildings were involved. Looking ahead several years we see these loans were in fact repaid though somewhat tardily. We can follow what happened in the case of one tenant, Stephen Peart, who paid the Earl £30 16s 8d in 1597. The total raised by the Earl in this way was £909.

Having solved his immediate financial difficulties the Earl took steps to discover just how much the manor was worth to him. This he did by employing a Kentish man, Samuel Peirse, to carry out a survey of every tenant's holding, which was completed in 1603. It is this survey which shows us how the whole township had been put into use during the past centuries.

The 1603 Survey

This survey is an excellent piece of work on all counts. Beautifully written in 17th century secretary hand, it goes into detail of every tenant's holding (Fig. 3). Unfortunately there is no sign of a map having existed, but an attempt has been made in the small one (Fig. 2) to show how the whole township was divided. We can leave out Grass Wood at this point as it was reserved entirely for the Lord of the Manor and his deer. There is no record of any tenant rights in it. If any customary practices had arisen and been allowed these did not appear in the records. The tenants did however have definite rights elsewhere. The map shows the main divisions. Most important were the three open, arable fields, West Field, Sedbur Field and East

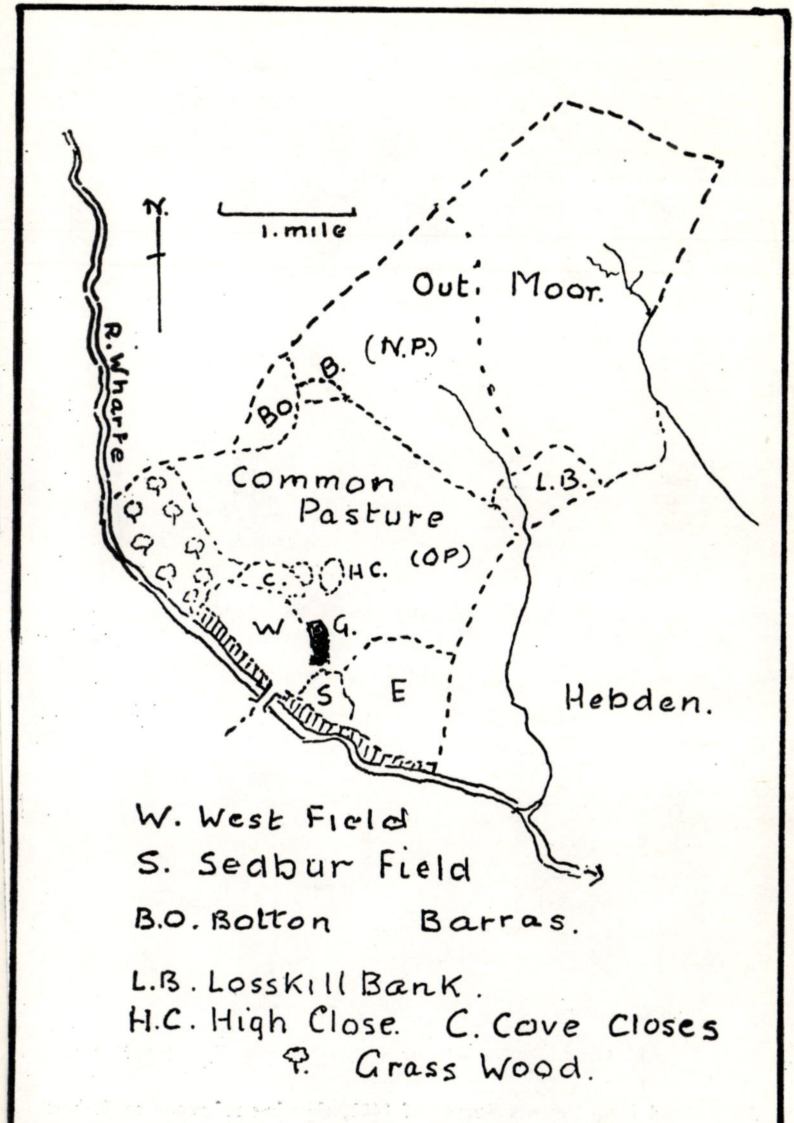

Fig. 2. Grassington Township about 1600.

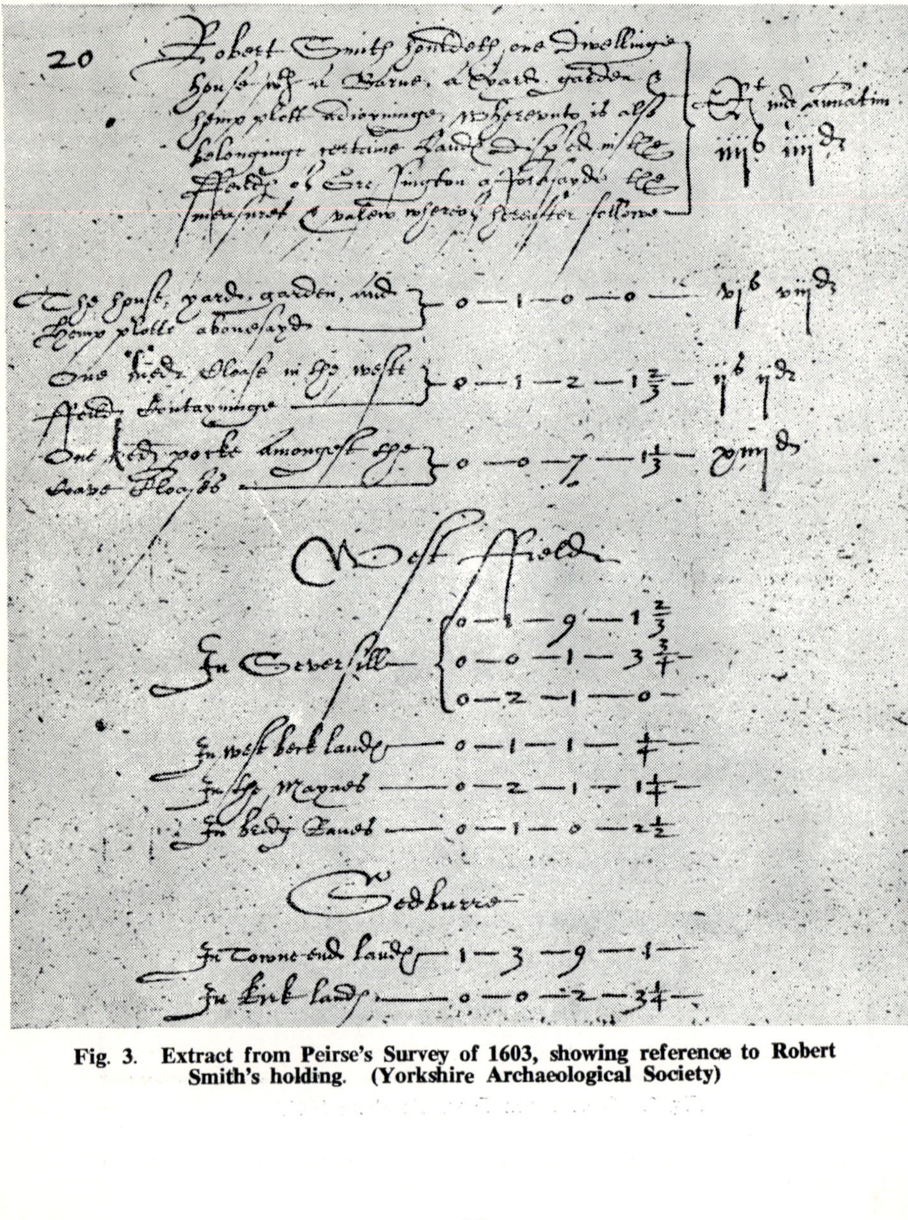

Fig. 3. Extract from Peirse's Survey of 1603, showing reference to Robert Smith's holding. (Yorkshire Archaeological Society)

Field, the Common Pasture and the Out Moor. In a few years a large piece was cut off the Moor, next to the Common Pasture, after which there was the Old Pasture and the New Pasture and the Moor. This is just indicated on the map. Most of the rest was enclosed land, always meadow or pasture except possibly small areas ploughed in war times. Meadows often had barns with hay stored above and cattle housed below in winter, and quite often a farm man and his family living in cramped quarters at one end. The most important enclosure was a very old one, High Close (Fig. 2), well within the bounds of the Common Pasture, taken in by the Lord from the best part at a very early date. The Cove Closes between the West Field and the Common Pasture were also early ones (see photograph—back cover, bottom). Parts of these and High Close, though providing very good grass, were allowed to grow hazel coppice until well into the 18th century for poles for many purposes. Most enclosures were made from the Lord's Waste with permission, but there were exceptions as we shall see. In nearly every case they had been made along one of the fixed boundaries, between the Moor and the Common Pasture, between one of the three fields and the pasture above, and so on, but when e.g. the East Field was extended, some early closes became, as it were, islands in a sea of arable. The occurrence of these islands is one of the main proofs of such extensions.

The arable fields were the most important part of the township since they produced the oats and other grains for bread, and barley for malt to make beer. Each tenant had scattered strips usually in all three fields, some more than 20 all carefully measured. Altogether there were 864, more than half in the East Field. For convenience these were divided into furshotts (called selions and other names in other districts). Each of the three fields was enclosed in a wall for a part of which each tenant was responsible, but the separate furshotts and strips were apparently temporarily fenced at special times as required. Hence one reason for the importance of coppice wood.

In the survey every man's holding is described in the same way, with the assessed value and rent for each section. In this account the value and rents have been omitted because the figures are completely unrealistic today. The areas need a little explanation. They are given simply as four figures, e.g. 1 - 2 - 9 - 3, which refer to acres - roods - daysworks - perches. The dayswork was a common measure at the time but as its meaning varied considerably from one district to another it is confusing. In this case it equals one-tenth of a rood. Four perches equal one dayswork, 10 daysworks one rood and 4 roods one acre, as today. In the document itself these areas are given in our Arabic figures but all the money, assessments and rents, are still in Roman figures.

For the following transcription the smallest holding is chosen for convenience (Fig. 3):

Robert Smith holdeth one dwellinghouse, a barn, yard garden and hemp plot adjoyning to which also belongeth lands and closes in the fields of Grassington.

West Field

In Seversill	(0 — 1 — 9 — $1\frac{2}{3}$	
	(0 — 0 — 1 — $3\frac{3}{4}$	
	(0 — 0 — 1 — 0	(The names on the left
In Westbecklands	0 — 1 — 1 — $1\frac{1}{4}$	are furshotts).
In the Mains	0 — 0 — 1 — $\frac{3}{4}$	
In Lady Banks	0 — 0 — 1 — $2\frac{1}{2}$	

Sedbur Field

In Town End Land	1 — 3 — 9 — 1
In Kirk Lands	0 — 0 — 2 — $3\frac{1}{4}$

East Field

In the doles beyond Wythe Closes 1 — 0 — 0 — 0

(These were rather poor meadow, a late extension of the field and were marked out by stones or enclosed).

Total of these	5 — 3 — 7 — $\frac{2}{3}$
of which Meadow	1 — 2 — 9 — 3
Arable	4 — 0 — 7 — $1\frac{2}{3}$

(In the Common Pasture	4 beastgates
(In the Oute Moor	10 sheepgates

The same Robert Smith hath also one smith's forge standing in the Town Gate for which he pays 2 shillings yearly.

(This smithy is at the entrance to the Square but at present unused — 1978).

Most tenants had one or more closes, entered before the strips.

The holdings of 30 tenants are described in this way and there are also five cottagers who had no arable strips or gates on the pasture and moor. The Lord of the Manor did not farm his own demesne; it was divided between his brother, Francis Clifford, and George Lister who lived at Grassington Hall. Francis Clifford and another tenant rented the cornmill on the riverside below Linton Church so that the Lord received a fixed profit, and had not to cope with the manorial tolls, the miller and the tenants with their corn.

The survey does not, unfortunately, give us any clue as to where all the tenants lived, but from later events and documents we can be sure that almost all of them lived in the village below the present Town Hall, with about six in an extension along the present Chapel Street. Each farmstead was compact in its own fold and had something in the way of croft, garden and in some even a small hemp plot. There would be much more open space than there is today.

Really outlying dwellings were rare and they were not so isolated as we are apt to think because so much of the traffic up and down the

Dale used high level tracks. Barras was the most important, an old enclosure on the edge of the moor, and in full use. Adjoining it was Botton, another older enclosure but its dwelling house was derelict, though the surveyor said if a tenant could be found it could be a good sheep farm. Several cottages were situated near the old high level road to Hebden, but, apart from Wythes or Wise House, they are either demolished or turned into barns.

There is one other item in the survey, described at length, which must be mentioned. That is Losskill Bank, the origin of which is explained. William Wrathall had been given permission to enclose 30 acres of the moor above the top of Hebden Gill. But he had agreed to accept £6 13s 4d from some of the other tenants and they enclosed 130 acres instead! The survey describes it as 'more than half lyngy and bentye ground and the rest reasonably good pasture'. The house which Wrathall had permission to build, or one on the same site, was built and occupied for a long time, but the scheming tenants soon lost their enclosure. A more blatant bit of unlicensed enclosure accounts for some of the small fields along the river below Linton Falls, but these seem to have been accepted by the Lord, as fait accompli, with a rent imposed.

The use which the Lord was to make of this survey brought about the birth of modern Grassington. The 17th century was to be in many ways the most interesting in all its history.

After the survey

An account of what happened after the survey has to be built up from documents which are quite detailed from the point of view of finance, but tell us very little of the human side of things. What a pity that keeping diaries was not a custom at that time!

It is quite clear that the Earl had planned a series of steps to raise money from Grassington. First there had been the mortgage, then the survey to find out exactly what each tenant's holding was worth, and now he started very quickly on the third move. This was to offer to all the tenants except the cottagers the freehold of their holdings and instalments of the purchase price were already being paid in 1604. A most important document, which appears to be a working copy of the original, gives all the information tabulated in three columns followed by others noting the amounts paid in the following years. The first three are headed:

1) Name of tenant.
2) Amount on mortgage acquitted.
3) Sums in gross.

Stephen Peart mentioned earlier was one for whom there are full details and a deed of sale. He had lent the Earl on the mortgage £30 16s 8d and he now had to pay £129 3s 4d in instalments. From this we find the purchase price of his holding was £160 from which the loan had been deducted and the mortgage acquitted.

By the deed which each tenant was given he received his holding by 'lease in fee simple for ever', in other words outright. He was now a freeholder with power to sell or bequeath his farm if he wished and to work it in his own way. But that was not the end of the manor for him. The Lord reserved his rights and Stephen still owed suit of court and mill. Matthew Hewitt who, although a rector of Linton, was also a freeholder in Kettlewell, was fined six pence for absence from the Lord's court in 1652. More unexpected than this was an 'ancient rent' to be paid to the Earl, a relic of the small levy made on all tenants. As the amount in this case was just two pence to be paid in equal parts at Pentecost and Martinmas if demanded, it had become merely an interesting legal figment. Other deeds about that time had more unexpected rents mentioned such as a peppercorn or, best of all, a red rose in the time of red roses. These were a relic of rents which freeholders had to pay instead of the boons of early manorial days, often in the form of eggs or hens. The amounts had not been increased to keep pace with inflation and for a long time had been only a token of the remaining influence of the Lord of the Manor.

No Lord of the Manor of Grassington has been known to demand these rents and the courts, and the mill, have passed away but the manor was never extinguished. The present corporate Lord, the Chatsworth Estates, still hold the mineral rights on the Moor though they have been leased from time to time.

Stephen Peart took longer than most to pay off his instalments, five years in fact; some did it in four and a few in three. Perhaps he was already enclosing some of his arable land which is mentioned in his deed as not yet enclosed, and so was short of money. The following years must have been a time of great opportunity for the new freeholders. Stephen met the challenge, but all were not so successful.

The New Freeholders

Thirty-two of the former tenants were now freeholders owning their land and buildings. But they were not entirely free of the manor, and the Skipton Manor Court records show that some of them were fined for not attending. As in most other places the power of the Manor Court had dwindled but that of the Quarter Sessions of the Justices of the Peace was growing. Maybe to the villagers the two appeared quite distinct in their functions, but to the historian, dependent on records, there seems to be overlapping. In addition the churchwardens had duties which at times were very mundane, such as paying parishioners for vermin such as fox-heads they had collected. One feels there must be, or have been, records somewhere of cases in Linton parish of some misdoings but both Quarter Sessions and Archdeacon's Court are silent. There was always a Grassington constable, responsible to the J.P. and the manor to some extent also.

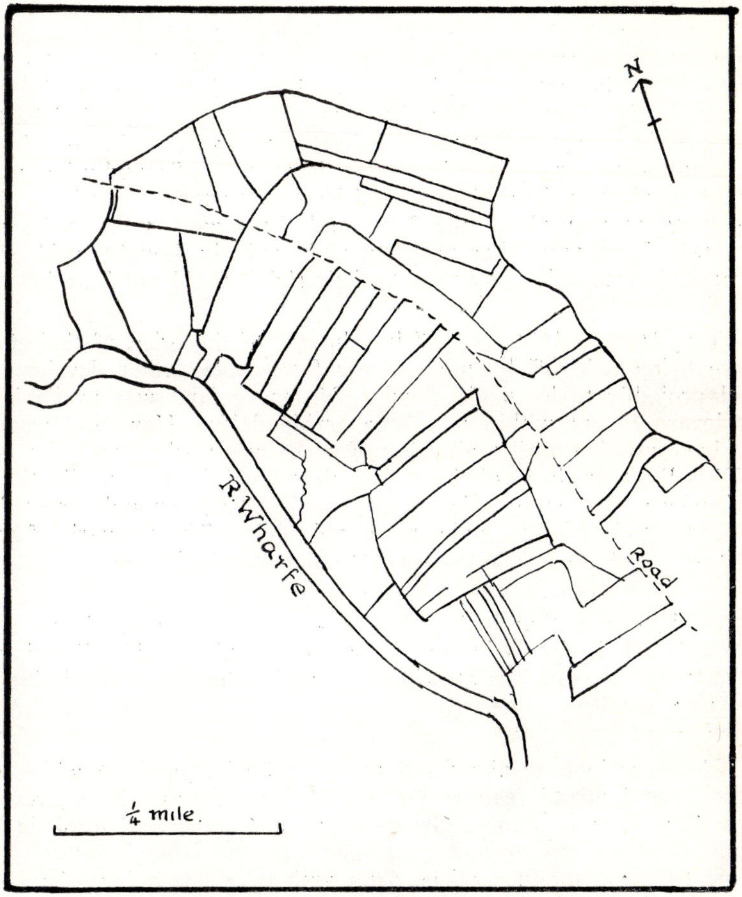

Fig. 4. Part of West Field, early 19th century.

Were they particularly efficient or did they occasionally turn a blind eye? It is difficult to imagine what sort of feeling there was in Grassington as the years went by. The year 1603 saw the end of Elizabeth's reign and then came the growing trouble, after James I's moderately calm years, of Charles I's conflict with Parliament, and then the Civil War and the Commonwealth, an unsettling background.

To begin with the new freeholders lost no time in getting on with other changes. As freeholders they had automatically right of pasture on the Lord's Moor which he had retained. But the Lord allowed two important developments. First a large area of the Moor was cut off to form the New Pasture, and this with the Old Pasture, the derelict farm of Botton and the illegally won enclosure of Losskil Bank were turned into four stinted pastures. Secondly he evolved schemes whereby freeholders could become owners of cattle or sheep gates on any or all of the four, and these gates were to be quite separate from any other property and could be bought, sold or bequeathed separately. As tenants their rights could not be sold.

From 1604 to 1606 or 1607 instalments of the price of their farms were being paid off by most of the farmers, so other developments had probably to be made slowly. No more land was available for enclosure except within the three arable fields. How that went on we have no clue until registering of deeds was made compulsory after 1700. By then it is obvious that there had been consolidation of strips by exchange or sale to get together large enough areas from the scattered strips to make reasonable fields. The network of walls, as it appears from a distance, was growing steadily (Fig. 4).

Another thing that had happened was the sale of land and gates, probably whole farms in some cases, to people outside Grassington. Investment in land was growing fast, and absentee landlords increasing as a result.

All this is looking ahead. Soon after 1603 something which may have caused mixed feelings among the farmers was the interest the new Lord of the Manor, George Earl of Cumberland, took in lead mining on the Moor and some parts of the stinted pastures. The subject of lead mining will be dealt with later but it is well to point out what is usually forgotten, that the destruction and actual poisoning of pasture through mining may have some bearing on the apparent financial failure of some farmers. They had no legal redress against the results of the Lord exercising his mineral rights on the Moor and stinted pastures.

On the other hand Grassington owed a great deal to the mines and miners in the build up of its character and subsequent history.

The Village in the 17th Century

THE VILLAGE as well as the general landscape was to be given a new look during this century. We know nothing of the buildings before 1600 except possibly Wesley's barn (Fig. 5). But there is a survey of Cracoe made in 1586 which sheds some light. The most substantial tenant there then was Stephen Kitching whose house and buildings are described as follows:

> 'One house being his firehouse of ffour paire of croks of ashe tymber and barn of ffour paire of croks of oake tymber latelye buylded one other house for hay of three paire of croks latelye buylded of oake tymber two other houses the one whereof is of three paire of ashe tymber croks and th'other of two pairs of ashe tymber.'

'Croks' now spelt 'crucks' were the main framework. A pair was made by cutting a long curved branch of ash or oak lengthways so that the two halves fastened together at the top made an arch. This was erected with the two ends standing on firm stones 16 feet apart; the different pairs were usually 12 feet apart, and held in place by a ridge pole. The rest of the building varied according to circumstances. In Grassington, where good timber must have been less plentiful than in Cracoe, the crucks would be shorter and standing on a low stone wall. Coppice wood would provide much of the walling with heather for thatching.

The first generation or two of freeholders would need time to recover from the cost of purchase and improvement and, before rebuilding their own homes, many would turn to improving their barns or building new ones on their enclosures. The first new house whose datestone remains is The Nook as it is called today, now divided, at the far end of Chapel Street. The date is hidden inside the porch, 1625. The next are 1631 and 1635, both difficult to find, but the majority are much later, possibly because of the unsettled period of the Civil War and Commonwealth. Unfortunately those stones which have initials incorporated are not as a rule much guide to occupiers because there has been much more removal of families than is generally thought. It just happens that the best datestone of all, that on the present Church House in the Square, 1694 with initials S P and A, is documented independently. It was built by Stephen Peart, a descendant of the one mentioned earlier, and his wife Alice. He lived on into the next century and when he died in 1709 an inventory of his personal estate was made.

Fig. 5. Wesley's Barn. (B. H. Wilkinson)

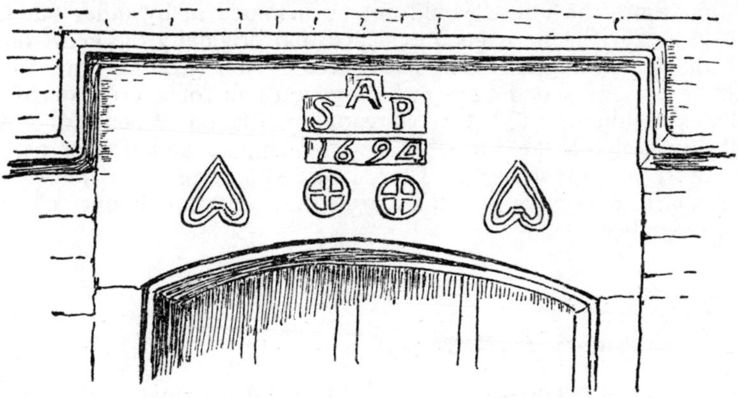

The house has been very much altered inside so that it is impossible to be sure how the various rooms fitted in. No size is given for any room but it is safe to say that 'small' would mean very small by our standards, and 'great' rather less than we expect. There were two floors, with parlours on the ground floor and chambers up above. Parlours were used as bedrooms frequently and any room might be used for storage purposes. The following are the main details of rooms and furniture in the order given. Floor covering and cutlery are not mentioned at all. They were little used then.

Kitchen — Brass pans and wood vessel.

Kitchen chamber — various storage vessels (for meal etc.).

Forehouse — Beef and bacon, a dresser and pewter, a clock, a glass case, 2 tables, a long settle and 6 chairs.

Great parlour — One bedstead and bedding, a cupboard and pewter, two tables and 4 chairs.

Little parlour — One bed and bedding, one press, one chest, one table, 2 chairs, one desk, two boxes, one form and pewter dishes.

Cellar — 6 barrels and one vat.

Great parlour chamber — 2 bedsteads and bedding, one livery cupboard, one table, one chest, 6 chairs and two forms.

Banister chamber — One bed and bedding and a chair.

Another chamber — One bedstead and bedding.

Great chamber (over the forehouse?) — One bed and bedding, 16 (?) chairs, 2 tables, two stands and one seeing glass.

Little chamber — One bed and bedding, one table, one chest and 6 chairs.

The Lad's chamber — One bed and bedding, one table and one chair.

A further list of linen, livestock including horses, oxen, other cattle and sheep, wool, hay, turf, carts, harness and oddments must have needed several barns or other outhouses which are not mentioned. At that time, the house would not be hemmed in by other buildings as it is today. There is good evidence that originally the Peart family had the big triangular area between the Hall grounds, the Square and the present Wood Lane, which gave room for a croft or fold as well as buildings. The two converted barns on Wood Lane were probably built on the site of those belonging to Stephen, or perhaps they were already rebuilt. There must still have been much more open space in Grassington than even the oldest inhabitants of today can remember.

The 17th Century in Retrospect

In following Stephen Peart to his life's end we have passed into the 18th century, but before we go any further it will be well to go back to 1600 and note one or two omissions. We have seen the great changes in land ownership and use. The development of the lead mining industry was briefly mentioned and much more will be told later. The Civil War was thought not to have disturbed Grassington seriously although Skipton Castle bore a long siege. Nothing so far has been said about the effects of the edicts of the rebel Parliament after it gained power in 1643. From then King Charles was king only in name. The course of the struggle ending in his execution in 1649 can be read in any history book. In it religion and politics were inseparably confused, though it is with neither of these that we are concerned here primarily. But the religious edicts of Parliament, especially after 1653, when Oliver Cromwell became Lord Protector, must have caused considerable heart-burning and apprehension, even so far away from the centre of government as Upper Wharfedale, for there were heavy fines for those reported for disobedience. Parliament and Cromwell were extremely Puritan and adopted the Scottish Presbyterian system of Church government and worship. The parish clergy of the Church of England, as well as the bishops and archbishops, lost all their administrative duties and the Book of Common Prayer was banned. In its place a book called the Directory was to be used, which gave directions for the ordinary services of the Church avoiding set forms but including sermons, long ones. Services for baptisms, marriages and funerals were forbidden: they were to be simple rites without the presence of a clergyman. In 1653 a new parish official was instituted, the Register, who was responsible for recording births, not baptisms, and marriages and burials. It was in connection with these changes that the people of Grassington must, in some families at least, have felt distress, for not only was the religious element cut out but so, according to the law, were the purely social celebrations, wedding cakes and so on. Two quotations from the Linton Parish Register give some details, even if the language is a bit strange, with blanks:

The Appointment of the Register

Forasmuch as William Wilson is certified to be at a publique meeting of the inhabitants of the parish of Linton. And forasmuch as . . . . has taken his oath before me this day faithfully and honestly to perform the office of parish Register . . . . according to the Act of this present Parliament for marriages and touching the Register thereof. And touching births and burials, I doe therefore hereby approve . . . . . . Given under my hand this day 22th of October 1653

(Signed) J. Roger Coates.

A Marriage Certificate

The intencion of marriage between George ffrankland of Griston and Margaret Tennant of Kettlewell was published 3 several market days in the Market Place att Skipton according to the Act of Parliament and the time limitted therein without any lett or contradiction viz the 7th 14th and 21st days of June and were married the 8th daye of July in the presence of
James Holey — By me
Richard Willson — (Signed) J. Ro Coates

J. Roger Coates was a Justice of the Peace. The marriage ceremony consisted merely of a declaration such as is made in Registry Office weddings, by the bridegroom and bride, followed by the completion of the marriage certificate, and must have seemed very inadequate to many people in Grassington.

One wonders what the attitude of Matthew Hewitt, one of Linton's rectors, was in these times. At the beginning of the Civil War he applied for the living at Gargrave whose vicar had joined the Parliamentary forces. A testimonial was sent on his behalf by well-known Linton people who had known him as curate, which read as follows:

> Mr. Hewitt hath been and is a faithful subject truly and discreetly jealous for the King, for the Church an orthodox and constant preacher, and such as by whom you may advance His Majesty's service.

Actually he remained at Linton and although there is no record of his appointment as rector, he remained until his death surviving all the difficulties of the Commonwealth by five years.

It was the same 'Mr. Hewitt' who by his will was to found Threshfield Grammar School to which Grassington boys were admitted and where they could win scholarships which he also instituted to St. John's College, Cambridge. Sad to relate very few were won by local boys. In the first twenty years of the school's existence only one Grassington boy went to Cambridge. He was William Topham whose family lived at the Hall. In 1694 he entered St. John's and eventually became Vicar of Flamborough.

A Note on Population

At the very end of the 17th century another Poll Tax was levied and the returns show only 19 married couples and 17 single persons, fewer than in 1379. The explanation may be found in a recently unearthed list of recipients of the Earl of Thanet's Charity in 1683. He, by marriage, had become Lord of Skipton Castle but in his benefactions for which he became famous he did not help only his own manors. A few years before this Poll Tax he distributed £100 in parishes over a wide area. At least 19 Grassington people received gifts of 1s or 1s 6d, much more worth while than it sounds today. Having received charity these people could claim to be paupers and therefore exempt from taxation and thus reduce the list of those assessed. The stigma attached to the name had not yet developed.

There is no list or other evidence remaining of the number of paupers in this village at this period. There were overseers of the poor who had power to levy a rate and later on there were six cottages owned by them for housing the homeless, but that was nearly a century later than the Earl of Thanet. By that time poverty was increasing. In the meantime there was a time of prosperity for most of the growing population.

The 18th Century

DURING this century there was great expansion in the lead mining and in the last decades a new textile industry was starting with Grassington and Linton mills both employing Grassington people. Farmers too were benefiting from both of these. Some of them, not so satisfied or successful as others, continued the sale of land, cattle and sheep gates, and even village houses. Many of the buyers were outsiders, but some local men began to build up sizeable estates. Two of these we know about because documents are available. One man was William Stockdale who in 1743 sold his house in the village, the whole house and farm of Barras, a half share in Grassington cornmill and a large number of arable and pasture lands and gates on the pastures. Barras was bought by the Vicar of St. Lawrence's Church, York, to augment the glebe. The other, Henry Marshall, master of Threshfield School, had acquired at least six houses in Grassington and a large number of closes and many cattle gates. William Stockdale seems to have left the district, though another branch of the family remained and now again owns Barras. Henry Marshall died and his estate was split up according to his will. One son who inherited a large share of Henry Marshall's estate sold most of it within a few years. One feels that here we have, for different reasons, two fathers who were disappointed men. What Stockdale did with the proceeds of his sale is not known. Perhaps he joined his son, who after Threshfield School and St. John's College became a vicar in Norfolk. Marshall did not in his will suggest that he had a very good opinion of at least one of his sons.

Whatever the reason for these transactions, they show how Grassington was gradually reverting to a village of tenant farmers, many with absentee landlords. One cannot help feeling that the tenants of 1603 who had gained for themselves the independence of freeholders would feel let down by their descendants had they known.

Lead Mining

Lead mining in Grassington township had been carried on since at least as early as the 15th century, as the two extracts from Fountains Abbey records show. These early workings can still be seen from the footpath crossing Lea Green, on the way to Conistone. They are little more than shallow opencast pits. There are useful books listed in the bibliography for those who want a more detailed account of the later industry. Only a brief summary is given here, sufficient to explain the effects it had directly and indirectly on the community as a whole.

It was not until George, Earl of Cumberland became Lord of the Manor that the industry came to life, though it had been carried on spasmodically and in a small way. The Earl was no stranger to lead mining and brought skilled men from his Derbyshire mines to work at Grassington. A few years later he built a smelt mill adjoining his cornmill on the River Wharfe. About a century later, in 1750, the Duke of Devonshire married one of the Clifford heiresses and came to be Lord of the Manor of Grassington. He began a great development plan for the industry involving a water-course to extend to the furthest mines, a long underground drainage channel to make the deeper pits workable, and a big new smelt mill, the Cupola, with the tall chimney, such a marked feature of the moor still, although for nearly 100 years it has not had to release the poisonous fumes out of harms way. Most of the other works and the spoilheaps have been so disturbed by the companies looking for barytes and fluorspar in recent decades that only an expert can understand the remains.

The Duke also greatly improved the highway between Grassington and Gargrave where he had a wharf on the Leeds and Liverpool Canal. When he died his successors carried on their interest in Grassington lead. It has been said that Chatsworth House was built out of Grassington lead.

Roads, Turnpikes and Others

The general increase in movement of people and goods in the 18th century led to a need for better roads. When we speak of a road today we assume a metalled highway more often than not, but these had not come into being at this time. A road was simply a way along which traffic moved and as it was unusual for them to be walled; pack ponies and wagons wandered about to avoid the worst ruts. Road mending was just a process of filling up ruts and holes with stones or even brushwood and soil, and was the responsibility of the villages. Lucky were villages like Grassington with stones in plenty. The mended parts were usually very narrow. All over the country groups of people were taking steps to improve the main highways. For this at first an Act of Parliament was necessary because of the inevitable cost and the need to acquire land, so the first step was to send a petition to Parliament. In 1754 the following was sent from the West Riding:

> Whereas the road leading from Wetherby . . . . Pateley Bridge, Hebden to Grassington in the County of York is very ruinous and dangerous to Passengers and for the most part very narrow that wheeled Carriages cannot pass along the same without greatest difficulty and cannot by the ordinary course provided by the Laws of the Realm for repairing the highways be

effectually mended widened and kept in repair and insomuch as the doing thereof will greatly lead to the Improvement of the Trade and Commerce of that part of the Country . . . .

This was the first part of the petition which had been submitted to Parliament and is quoted in the preamble to the Act which gave permission for the formation of a trust to construct a new highway, with toll-bars or turnpikes at intervals, at which tolls were collected to pay for the construction and upkeep. The 191 signatories of the petition formed the trust. They were the owners of land through which the new road was to run or which bordered it, and included farmers like Anthony Dean of a long established Threshfield and Grassington family and more than one of the Alcocks, an important Skipton banking and business family who for some time owned Grassington House.

The new road usually followed the course of the old one more or less, but the Grassington one as far as Hebden was made much lower down, with a marked double bend to go round old enclosures. There was no tollgate on the Grassington section. The list of tolls is interesting for the light it sheds on the traffic of the period. It begins: 'For every coach, landau, hearse drawn by 6 horses, 1s 9d'. Then come smaller vehicles for passengers, and after them wagons. Those carrying coals, lime, peat, turf going or returning empty and drawn by five or more horses or oxen were subject to reduced tolls if they were going backwards and forwards from local pits, mines or quarries. There were a lot of exemptions from tolls, for farm produce, road mending material, people going to church or to funerals, and there were no tolls at all on election days. The Royal Mail was always free.

Turnpike roads were not popular with everyone and it is recorded in books on the subject that trains of pack ponies often kept to the old roads where possible, to avoid the tolls and the increasing traffic.

No other turnpikes touched Grassington. The Duke's improved road from Gargrave was joined by a very late and short one from Skipton to Cracoe in 1853, and reached the village over the Wharfe bridge, correctly called Linton Bridge. (Though one end is in Threshfield and the other in Grassington, the whole is in the old parish of Linton). This bridge is well documented since 1600 when it was, according to a J.P's report to Quarter Sessions, 'very ruinous and oak trees are needed'. Fortunately by that time oak trees of the required size were very scarce and the bridge was rebuilt in stone, but very narrow. In 1780 it was widened and in 1825 it was extensively improved to remove the central hump back, the signs of which can still be seen from the fields on each side.

Before these later improvements the road from the bridge up the dale turned immediately left avoiding the steep hill up to the village and joined the line of the present Wood Lane near the barn now marked on maps as Rilston Hill Laithe, but which was known in 1603 as Resting Hill. Continuing through Grass Wood as shown on Ogilby's road map of 1675, through Conistone and on through Kettlewell it crossed over to Coverdale, Middleham and finally Richmond. It is in fact part of a road shown by Ogilby as a through route from London of which he shows the whole length. Grassington however was not conveniently situated to benefit. It is doubtful if many coaches used the complete length and it was not a regular route for mail coaches. Ogilby gives the distance from London to Grassington as 231 miles.

Another surprising road from Grassington is a continuation of the turnpike from Pateley Bridge. It is given in Mogg's revision of 'Paterson's Roads' in 1812 as a through road from York to Lancaster. From Grassington it went by Threshfield, Skirethornes and Malham Moor, having joined Mastiles Lane. Part of this is no more than a bridle track now.

An interesting old way, mentioned in an early chapter, is that which runs, first as a path, straight up from the Wharfe bridge up the steps of a 'flight' of lynchets, then on new roads but still straight ahead up what is called Moody Stye to the top of the village. Stye means a ladder and that is intelligible, but who or what was Moody?

The Lost Eleven Days

One happening in 1752 accounts for an annual event whose occurrence puzzles some people in Grassington every October, the Feast. Originally, by the 1282 market charter, a fair was to be held at Michaelmas, September 29th, the feast day of St. Michael's Church. But in 1752 the European calendar had got out of step with the sun's apparent movements and to get it right, as in other countries, it was decided to cut eleven days containing no important dates out of the calendar for that year. Consequently, when what should have been September 29th came, it was officially October 11th. However, Grassington people refused to accept this and pleaded 'Give us back our eleven days'. But in vain! Since then the Feast has always been celebrated, and the few remaining stalls, etc., still appear, eleven days after the Church's Feast of St. Michael.

There had already been one change in the calendar in 1752. January 1st had become New Year's Day for the first time instead of March 25th (Lady Day). To avoid mistakes during the first three months official documents, such as the Parish Register, had the year written 1752/3.

The 19th Century Background

IN the first half of the 19th century Grassington reached a peak of activity and prosperity which resulted in a continued growth in population. Not only were farming, lead mining and the textile industry full of life but things of the mind and spirit were taking shape too in the Nonconformist chapels, the Mechanics Institute, the National School and at least two friendly societies. It is fortunate that the census taken every ten years coincided in 1851 with this peak (Fig. 6).

The second half shows an even more rapid fall than the previous rise, owing to a virtual collapse of the lead mining and a serious decline in the textile industry, which must have caused difficulties for the farmers also. But as the years passed, Grassington began to find new interests which led eventually to the very profitable tourist industry, as well as openings for employment further afield.

It is against this general background that the different aspects of the village history during the century are described. It will help to keep things in perspective if we remember that in one family it was not unknown for father to be a miner, mother and a daughter mill operatives, and a son working as a farm man.

The Last Days of Lead Mining

The mechanisation of the mines with the water courses and drainage level, which had begun with the Duke of Devonshire about 1750, was carried on and new grounds opened and others re-opened. The pony level leading down to veins at Yarnbury, with the date 1828 on the entrance arch, is there for anyone to see. Near at hand are some of the latest bell pits but most of the spoil tips round about have been worked for fluorspar and barytes in recent years, and the old mine buildings have mostly been demolished. At Yarnbury on the Moor Road only the smithy remains with a roof, but the mine manager's house and two cottages have recently been restored.

In 1851 the industry was at its height. The Cupola smelt mill was working and about 140 men from Grassington were employed on the various processes. Then lead ore was found in Spain and America in large amounts and with a much higher silver content than in the Pennines and this flooded the market. Only a few mines were able to keep going and only for a few years. Families began to leave the village and the population graph shows what happened. The dramatic decline would have been even more depressing for the village if the textile mills had not continued, though rather spasmodically, for a time.

The Textile Industry

The textile industry in the district was started by J. and W. Birkbeck and Co. about 1790. The three Birkbeck brothers, John, William and George, had already opened a mill at Addingham and others elsewhere. (George was a sleeping partner, being a scientist first at Glasgow University where his courses for working men led to the foundation of Mechanics' Institutes and later in London where Birkbeck College was named after him). In 1792 Hargreaves and Co. were working Linton Mill for worsted manufacture and in 1814 Birkbecks, still the owners, built a bridge over the falls for the benefit of the workpeople living in the cottages by the mill, shortening the walk to the shops for them, and to the mill for those coming from Grassington to work.

Grassington Mill is first mentioned in the 1840s when Thomas Mason & Co. held the tenancy. In the 1851 census returns Thomas

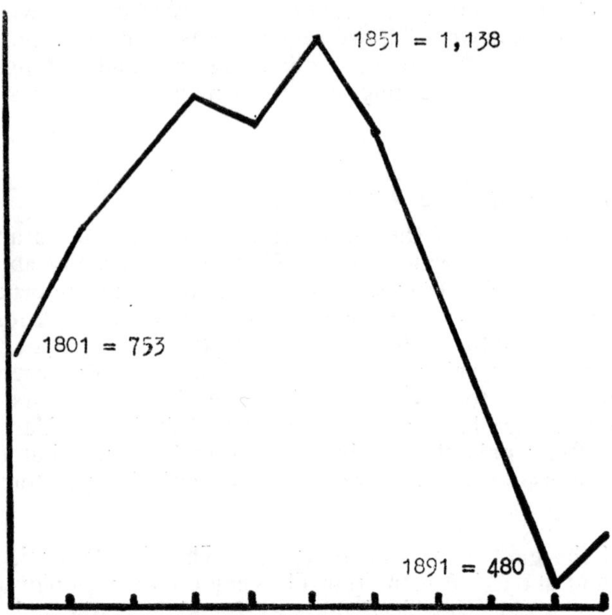

Fig. 6. Population of Grassington, 1801–1901.

Mason is given as a worsted manufacturer, born in Addingham, and a younger man, William Cockshott, is described exactly in the same way. It seems likely that Cockshott was connected with Linton Mill.

By this time the Birkbeck brothers had died and the company was carried on through trustees who in 1856 advertised all the company's local estate for sale. From this time ownership of the two mills is rather uncertain except for a few definite dates. Henry Alcock & Co. were working Grassington in 1860 for cotton spinning but the 1861 census mentions worsted and cotton manufacture without in most cases saying at which mill. In 1878 Grassington is referred to as a worsted mill and confusion increases. Linton was in a poor way for some time round about 1890. Grassington, according to Bailey Harker, was much more active, but by 1894 after several years' tenancy by members of the Holdsworth family, it is given in the Land Tax lists as no longer working and unoccupied. Linton carried on spasmodically and did not finally close down till 1959. For a time only a few weavers had been employed on making rayon lining material, until for the last week only one woman was employed.

That is the story, though incomplete, of the main textile manufacture in the district, but there are two other side-lines which should be mentioned.

In the 1603 survey 14 tenants were shown having hemp plots in among their farm buildings and their houses. These must have been very small indeed, not many square yards. Others had gardens in which hemp could have been grown also. This means that there must have been a domestic spinning and weaving industry on a very small scale, producing a coarse form of linen for dress or household purposes, in the days before cotton was imported. Nothing else is known about it; no mention has been found in any documents. Maybe, with a weekly market, visiting chapmen may have brought ready-made material, so letting the ground be used for growing vegetables which had become more popular before the mills opened.

The second omission from the main story was made to avoid complicating an already confused account. There was a third mill, very small and very short lived, at Town Head, in a building still known as Scaw Gill. In 1792 the land on which it stands was leased to William Hargreaves & Co. of Linton Mill. As a very small stream runs down the field there may have been a suggestion to build a mill there but there clearly was not one in existence, from the terms of the deed. However one was built, but by whom is not revealed. The small wheel pit is still there, though covered. In 1810 a building known as Scawgill was sold, described as 'formerly a cotton mill in the occupation of Samuel Gill and lately of Richard Chester but now divided into two cottages.' And two cottages it remained for a long time, though part was used as a butter factory for a time. Hargreaves & Co. may have built the mill but the essential deed is missing. They cannot seriously have thought any possible competition dangerous. The mill was not a success judging from its short life, which cannot have been as long as 20 years.

The Inclosure Award

The 19th century for farmers indubitably began in 1792, with the Inclosure Award which caused greater changes than any except the sales following the 1603 survey. Four years earlier all the holders of gates on the four stinted pastures of Grassington had been summoned to a meeting to discuss the proposal to exchange each man's beast and sheep gates for allotments of land in these pastures. These were to be walled and become the property of the allottees to keep, sell or bequeath as desired, subject only to the Lord of the Manor's mineral rights and others, as in all freeholders deeds.

The necessary act of Parliament was passed and commissioners and a surveyor appointed to draw up the award. A very difficult task it must have been to try to allot fairly land of very different qualities, proportional to the number of gates held. Area was by no means the main consideration. Consequently some allotments were small but good pasture, others large but not so good. Some were very long and narrow, usually in order to get access to water and it is almost inevitable that not all people were satisfied (Fig. 7).

The award included detailed instructions as to how the walls were to be built and by whom and set a time limit of twelve months for their completion. Access roads were arranged and small areas set aside for the supply of stones for walling as well as other quarries for limestone for burning. Many of the new allotments were badly in need of lime dressing and a lot of small lime kilns were built and worked by men who had suitable limestone outcrops on their land. Coal was easily available from Threshfield Moor, of poor quality but excessive ash just mixed with the burnt lime and did no harm. The limed land soon began to show a brighter green and farmers' kilns worked well and the lime found a ready market.

Before long these improved pastures could feed more animals than the beast and sheep gates had done and they began to take on a new look with considerable numbers of black Scotch cattle bought at the big fairs held on Malham and Boss Moor. The Malham Moor fair had been built up by a Skipton grazier called Birtwhistle and, as the big industrial towns increased in size, the demand for Scotch beef grew likewise. Now the Grassington farmers were able to take and fatten some cattle for which they had not been allowed to use their beast gates. Now they could do as they pleased.

But the award caused big expenditure and labour on wall building in particular and the sale of new allotments began almost immediately and the proportion of absentee landlords increased. By 1846, when the Tithe Commutation Act award was made, only about one in six of all the properties listed was owner occupied or worked. Almost certainly some of the smaller transactions which appear as sales were

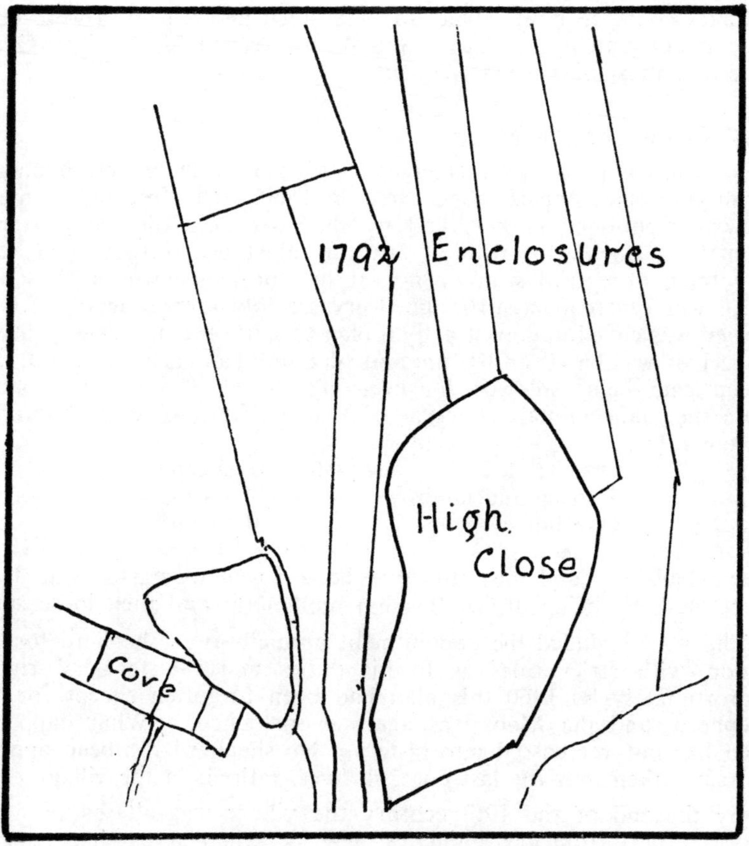

Fig. 7. 1792 enclosures surrouding High Close.

in reality mortgages which could be paid off after a time, and there was a noticeable move on the part of some miners to acquire small fields and build up smallholdings as a very sensible second string in a fitful industry. There is more than one family in Grassington who came a few generations ago for lead mining but stayed to farm.

The farmers in many cases were not slow to see another line of business open to them in the first half of the 19th century. Population was rising rapidly, housing was inadequate and most farmers had crofts, or folds as they were called, in which one or more small cottages could be built. One up, one down and a lean-to were considered adequate for a farm hand or miner and his family. Overcrowding must have been frequent.

The Stinting of the Moor

Naturally among all the changes in this period, there were bound to be disputes and one such occurred in 1860. The freehold farmers, as was mentioned earlier, had by their freehold the right to put animals on the Moor without any official stint. If there had been any form of agreed stint or not, it had broken down in 1860 and there was severe over-stocking. Very sensibly a meeting of all concerned was called and eventually a plan to settle the matter was drawn up. This was based on the amount of Land Tax each man paid, one sheep gate being allowed for every £1 9s 0d of tax paid. Sheep were the main animals concerned but ohers were allowed at the following rates:

One beast	equal to 5 sheep
3 sheep and lambs	to 5 sheep
One horse	to 10 sheep
10 geese	to 1 sheep

Geese had been and may still have been driven to market with their feet 'shod' by being driven through molten tar and then loose sand.

The plan included the appointment annually of a shepherd for the Moor, with strict rules as to his duties and the farmers' rights. Unfortunately by 1960 this plan had been forgotten except for the shepherd, and the Moor was again over-stocked. What happened then has not yet passed into history. No shepherd has been appointed since then, but the last one still lives, retired, in the village.

By the end of the 19th century the village was altered in many ways. Apart from new buildings, new ideas had taken shape, social, religious and educational, and we must go back to 1800 to see how they began.

Nonconformity in Grassington

In the earlier chapters we have noticed that during the long years of religious persecution there were no known Grassington martyrs except William Dean. But we cannot imagine a community having no dissidents through all those troublous times. No records, parish or village, tell us anything, but persecution in any serious form ended in 1698 after which Nonconformist places of meeting could be licensed. Nothing however is known for nearly another hundred years, until John Wesley stopped on two occasions in 1780 and 1782 to preach to Grassington on his way from Skipton to Pateley Bridge.

In his diary Wesley tells how he found a great crowd waiting for him at 10 o'clock in the morning, which shows that he was expected, and that he already had a following. He is reputed to have stood outside the old building now often called Wesley's barn, into which he no doubt retreated when it 'rained much' after he finished. No results of his visit are known directly, but in 1801 Grassington was mentioned in Skipton Circuit lists as having a Mission, and in 1809 a minister was appointed. They must then have begun to plan their own chapel, for in 1811 it was ready and opened, though later additions were made.

The Independents had as yet no chapel but had held house meetings and some had occasionally gone to worship at Winterburn, six miles away, the oldest Nonconformist chapel anywhere near. When the Methodists planned their chapel, the Independents were stirred to ask the Idle Academy for help, and students from there began to come to preach. As a result the house meetings were overcrowded and by a great effort an Independent Chapel was planned, built and opened. The first service was held on Christmas Day 1811.

In 1837 the Methodist congregation lost a considerable number of its members who broke away to build their own chapel and join the Primitive Methodist Connexion. That building in Chapel Fold was given up in 1908 and became an ordinary house, and a new chapel was built next to the Devonshire Institute. This also was given up about 1948 and, having been pulled down stone by stone, was rebuilt in Broughton Road, Skipton. Very recently that too was demolished and not replaced.

The Independents carried on but had difficulties, as no doubt the Methodists also had, caused by the great decrease in population. In time they became known as Congregational, the name referring to the control exercised by each congregation over its own affairs. This control the Grassington congregation, though small, has recently insisted on maintaining by deciding not to join the United Church. It is a pity that in their secluded graveyard so many gravestones have not endured the test of time. They might have told us much, but it is an unexpectedly peaceful spot in a not now so quiet village.

Friendly Societies and Others

In the early 19th century there was a rapid growth in the number of friendly societies, mainly in the industrial areas for the purpose usually of encouraging thrift among the workers. The discovery of a little tattered booklet brought to light the fact that such a Friendly and Charitable Society was founded in Grassington in 1808 and was still in action in 1858. The cover and end papers give the name of the Society, the two dates and the names of the three officials financially responsible, called stewards. The namesake of one of these, Thomas Joy, the last Grassington Moor shepherd, is still active in the village today. The rest of the book is filled with over 60 complicated rules drawn up in an Act of Parliament controlling such societies. There is no clue as to whether or not the society had any activities beyond collecting weekly subscriptions and paying out benefits in time of need.

The Oddfellows may have started early but the first dated mention is in 1878. They are still in existence and meet regularly. Other groups of a different kind which met over considerable but rather vague periods were the Band of Hope, the Brass Band and the Boys Brigade. The last two are well remembered by some of the older residents. Nowadays the number of organisations is legion.

The Mechanics Institute

In the mid 19th century Mechanics Institutes were being formed in many places where there were large numbers of 'mechanics', which then included craftsmen and other manual workers. One was founded in Grassington in 1841 for the benefit mainly of workers at the lead mines and mills, but all were eligible. Records do not begin till 1846 and are very inadequate. From them it is impossible to do more than give brief glimpses at very irregular intervals. Only one activity persisted throughout, reading, both library and newspapers, the newsroom being open from 10 a.m. to 10 p.m.

In 1846 a delegate to the Yorkshire Union of Institutes' A.G.M. reported on Grassington: "The Institute is now recovering from a languid period'. No more reports were made in person to the Union till 1855. That year the Duke of Devonshire built at his own expense a special meeting place for the Institute, which so far had met in hired rooms. Membership soared to 160 under the leadership of three men known in other positions. Stephen Eddy, the president, was the Duke's chief mine agent: William Cockshott, vice-president, was manager for the Birkbeck Company which owned both mills at that date. The secretary was master of Threshfield School and parish clerk, John Harker, who for 35 years was an active personality in the parish, commemorated in stained glass windows in the church. Yet by 1857 membership had halved and the minute book is left unused until 1871 when a new one was started. John Harker had died in 1860.

In 1878 the Duke added a new reading room and others, and from then onwards the Institute is shown as much better organised and purposeful. In 1891, as a result of a public meeting, a course of ten lectures on agriculture drew very large audiences, and classes in dairying were discussed but replaced by more lectures. By this time a large number of 'mechanics' had left the district and the farmers had again become the main element in the community. These years appear from the books to have been the best of the Institute's history, with increasing bookings also of the rooms for other activities, from Boys Brigade to bazaars. In 1896 the building was conveyed by the Duke of that date to the recently inaugurated civil Parish Council, but the Devonshire Institute Committee has continued throughout to administer the use of the building with absolute right to the use of the reading room. Since then it has become generally known as the Town Hall, a pretentious and misleading name perhaps. Yet Grassington has been a 'ton', the Old English form of the word, for over a thousand years!

The name 'Mechanics' was quietly dropped as more and more organisations began to use the rooms. A final addition to the building was made in 1923, the large hall and foyer, paid for by public subscription. Not many villages of the size of Grassington have such an imposing and useful institution. Looking up at it people think of it as mainly the gift of the Duke of Devonshire. Few realise that the Mechanics Institute movement grew out of ideas formulated by George, the youngest of the three Birkbeck brothers, whose company founded the two textile mills (as told in the section on the mills). He died in the year this Institute was started, but it is possible that, though mainly a sleeping partner, he had been interested in the early life of the mills, so near Settle where he was born.

The National School

By 1845 Grassington had three Nonconformist chapels, a Mechanics Institute, and the parish church had been made more easily accessible by the bridge at Linton Falls. It was high time for a school to be built. The population was rising rapidly and, apart from short-lived 'dame' schools of doubtful quality, there was no school for girls. Threshfield School did not become a primary school for both boys and girls till 1876. So financial help was sought from the National Society whose object was the education of boys and girls according to the teaching of the Church of England. There were also local subscribers, and a school was built. The original building erected in Wood Lane in 1845 is still used but is supplemented by new buildings off Hebden Road opened in 1970.

The old building originally had three rooms used by the teacher or teachers as living accommodation. In 1857 it was partly furnished for Miss Rogers, who received £45 a year salary. Ten years later, on the appointment of Miss Coulson at £72 per annum, it was supplied with almost every necessity, including 14 yards of coconut matting, two egg cups, a rocking chair and a looking glass. Unfortunately, just before this, according to a curate's letter, the school, like the Mechanics Institute, had gone through 'a languid period', and had lost the government grant for efficiency, but obviously a new start had been made in spite of the depression which just then was beginning to affect the life of the village.

It is difficult to imagine how this school affected the community. There are no available records for the first eleven years, but it must have been an influence for good. The building was soon found to have a double purpose, being used for Sunday evening services and for any weekday meeting connected with the church. This use as church rooms continued until 1924 when the present Church House in the Square was bought for the purpose. Since Stephen Peart died there in 1709 this house had seen many owners and been altered inside, and now more changes were made, chief of which was a screened alcove with altar, consecreated for use on weekdays and also Sundays in winter.

The old school building in Wood Lane is now regarded as old fashioned. The whole of it is used for classes but rarely for other purposes, but the school itself flourishes and is an important part of the village. Its old log book covering from 1869 to 1920 contains much of interest and some items, mostly bearing on village life, are given here:

1866. March 14th. School closed because of a church service, it being a fast day for the cattle plague now raging.

1871. Six girls gone to a school for young ladies in the village. They want to learn needlework.

1877. 13 children admitted from the school in the village given up. The girls admitted from the Dame School are very untidy and careless.

1879. May. Two girds have gone to work half time at the factory.

1884. May. Pupil teachers began to have lessons from 7 a.m. to 8 a.m.

1888. Nov. 9th. Richard and Martha Birch (from Barras) absent all week because of bad weather (and for several more weeks).

1895. June. A good many children absent. Needed at home because so many visitors in Grassington.

1900. June 7. Children took part in procession at the cutting of the first sod of the railway.

1911. On the roll 89. (1917: 106).

1912. Inspector's report. The use of slates and slate pencils to be deprecated.

1917. A good number of children have left to work in the factory and none at farm work. (13 years of age).

1920. His Majesty's Inspector reports that a large number of children come to school without handkerchiefs.

Another subject occurring repeatedly in the log-book is a result of Threshfield School being free whereas 'school pence' had to be paid at Grassington until 1904 when the County took Grassington over. There are numerous entries telling of children transferring to Threshfield apparently when money was short and coming back when things improved. There is no suggestion in the book that there was any difficulty about this.

Finally it is from the log-book that we have information about the holding of Grassington fairs. Originally there was only one, instituted by the charter in 1282, held at Michaelmas, the remnants of which are still known as the Feast. But over the centuries other fairs had developed, until there were four. In the log-book it is stated year after year that either the school was closed or that the attendance was poor owing to the fair. The dates vary and the number dropped to one in spring, last mentioned in 1906. Rather strangely the Feast is never mentioned. Possibly it was a traditional holiday time for the whole village. By 1906 the days of more frequent but smaller fairs in various places had dawned, arranged as experience directed and not just according to tradition. Motor transport for sheep and cattle has altered the picture again.

The Liverpool Warehouse

In 1848 William Cockshott, of Linton Mill, was worried about the inadequate shopping facilities for his workpeople, and he decided to open a shop in Grassington Market Place. The owners of the mill, J. & W. Birkbeck & Co., had built 20 cottages by the mill for workpeople and a bridge over the falls to take them quickly to the village and to shorten the walk for the numerous Grassington people employed. By 1861 this shop had become the Liverpool Warehouse at the top of the Square and sold all kinds of goods, taking advantage of the overseas trade of Liverpool and the Leeds and Liverpool Canal, with railway transport developing rapidly. In the census returns of that year, 1861, a young man, unmarried and 33 years of age, Fieldhouse Holmes, was given as living at the Liverpool Warehouse with a young boy apprentice, while he himself was assistant shopman (see front cover photograph).

William Cockshott, who had appeared in the 1851 census as a worsted manufacturer and head of his household in Grassington, has been demoted to second place and he is now a draper. His much younger sister Arabella is now the head of the household and a grocer and draper. In the interval the Birkbeck firm had sold both mills after which Linton Mill had a very chequered career. The days of small village factories were very nearly ended and Cockshott may have become redundant, as we say nowadays, and gone bankrupt. He was only 53. Holmes must have married soon after 1861 as in 1866 he married Margaret Hall and is described then as a widower. He became the proprietor of the shop so it is tempting to think that perhaps he married Arabella. He and the Cockshotts were all born in Addingham and he and Arabella were much of an age. Whoever his first wife was, the marriage was tragically short.

Fieldhouse Holmes, or Fiel-us as he was called locally, was still advertising his business in 1890 when he was 63. After his death his son, always spoken of as Bertie, carried on. Eventually, about 1920, the business closed and the premises became a cafe. More could be said about it, but a paragraph by a Craven Herald contributor in the '30s looking back describes the shop as he knew it and sums it up well.

> There one could buy anything from pins to bacon — a kind of 'Selfridges of the Dales'. It had imposing ledgers, high stools, and tobacco coiled on the counter like pigtails of Georgian seamen, and a composition of old-fashioned odours never to be forgotten.

Being a man the writer was probably not interested in the drapery but the mention of Selfridges indicates that it was included. Several people who shopped there in their schooldays remember particularly the long strands of black liquorice also coiled on the counter. A bill among the Mechanics Institute papers adds candles, lamps, soap, brushes, blacklead and soda to the list of goods sold. Stocktaking must have been a wearisome business!

Some Grassington Personalities

Several writers have told at length the story of Tom Lee, the murderer hanged in 1766, and of Thomas Airey, a much more worthy character, whose prowess as an actor and the inspirer of Grassington theatre brought him fame throughout the dale and in Skipton in the early 1800s. (See 'Old Skipton' by Dr. Rowley).

Three others more recent have not been given so much notice but are not forgotten. In chronological order they are Bailey J. Harker, John Crowther and Christopher, generally known as Kit, Chapman.

Bailey Harker was born in 1844 in Grassington, the son of a tailor, and he became a Congregational minister. This calling took him away from the village for long periods as he never had a local church or one anywhere in the Dales. Yet his claim to remembrance lies mainly in his two small books about the district but also in his investigations and finds among the prehistoric sites in Grass Wood, High Close and elsewhere. He was reputedly the first to recognise Gregory fort in Grass Wood as something man made. His two books were 'Rambles in Upper Wharfedale', writen in Wales when he was only 25, and 'Grassington: the Buxton of Wharfedale' in 1890 when he had a church in Bolton, 25 years later.

Well before 1890 he must have come into contact with John Crowther. We know he was once without a church for two years and must have come home at intervals. Crowther was born in Bradford in 1858 but his mother was born in Kettlewell where he had an uncle who was an ardent botanist. The young John, probably through his uncle's influence, had already gained a considerable knowledge of herbs when he became apprenticed to Dr. Anthony who had an apothecary's shop in Grassington Main Street (Fig. 8). Here his interest in botany and other aspects of the countryside were helped by his need to travel up and down the dale in pursuit of business and he had progressed sufficiently to take over the shop when the doctor died in 1884. In time he became noted as a cow doctor and incidentally learnt much of the geology and archaeology of the country. It was these interests which drew the two men together (see 'Old Yorkshire Dales').

By 1901 Bailey Harker had already made a considerable collection of flints and other artifacts which he asked the Mechanics Institute committee to house and exhibit. He was then at a Bolton church and found in a nearby museum some suitable show cases being sold cheaply. Some years later most of this collection went to swell

Fig. 8. Main Street in 1897. (B. H. Wilkinson)

Crowther's own in a special hut Crowther built near his house. Unfortunately there is some confusion about the dates of the activities of the two men due to conflicting records but this does not really matter; they worked happily together but were very different.

Harker was quite ready to fill in gaps in knowledge with imaginings; Crowther had a scientific mind, anxious to find the right answer. He joined outside societies and met well known scientists. Among these Professor Boyd Dawkins came to see what Crowther had to show him and he and others respected him for his intelligent work and helped him with advice.

But there were still other sides to Crowther's life. He was very anxious that young people should grow up with a knowledge and appreciation of the countryside so he held an informal club for them in his house and took them out to see things. Later he founded a Boy Scouts troop. He was also keenly concerned with the welfare of the village and was largely instrumental in getting electricity and sewerage. In 1911 he was publicly thanked for his successful campaign. Yet for all that there is nothing left in Grassington as a memorial. He presented his museum collection including Bailey Harker's from the Institute to the Craven Museum two years before he died. Only Bailey Harker's beaker from a burial mound on High Close was given separately. More recently another collection of flints, that of Arthur Waters, has gone to join Crowther's. There is no memorial to Crowther in Grassington. He was buried in Conistone churchyard where he had already erected to his son, Maurice, killed in the first world war, a memorial near which he himself wished to lie. A small book long out of print called 'Silva Garrs' contains much of what he wrote about the district with articles by others as well.

Christopher Chapman (Kit to most people) was of a very different type from either of the above, but probably in his day better known than either of the others to all sorts and conditions of men, concerned as he was with transport in the dale for over fifty years, first at Buckden and then at Grassington. For some years he ran the Buckden to Skipton horse mail and then came to Grassington to take over the business carried on for several generations of the Airey family from the house in the Square, now Church House, with stables then adjoining. This included the contract for H.M. Mails but regular services besides these were run to Buckden, Arncliffe, Hebden and Bolton Abbey, and visitors could be met from trains or taken on pleasure drives over a wide area. Eventually over 45 horses were employed, many of them pastured beyond the village, clattering noisily up and down the cobbled Main Street night and morning. Then in 1907 Chapman bought the first motor bus to be seen for miles around and ran it from Grassington railway station to Buckden. His youngest son Robert became the usual driver and the writer of this account remembers vividly the loading up of visitors' luggage and the stark simplicity of the vehicle in 1908: no hood, the climb up into each separate row of seats, but apparently sound and reliable machinery. Like the horses, it got there on time.

Gradually more motor buses were used, each, it was said, replacing nine horses, until a much larger organisation was needed. Then Chapmans, Christopher and his four sons, sold out to the West Yorkshire Road Car Company, and their house, for some time a Temperance Hotel, was sold to the church authorities. The last of the sons, Robert, who drove the first bus in 1907/8, died in 1950.

Local people will naturally think of many other memorable folk who might be added to these. Perhaps a word may be added about one who only a few years since became part of history, Jim Ward, who for over 40 years carried on the high standards of the Chapmans as driver, inspector and, for some years, was in charge of Grassington Bus Station. It would have been difficult to replace him, but fortunately in this connection the bus service had shrunk so much that no one was needed.

The 20th Century

WE have already stepped over the line from the 19th into the 20th century but history is like a well-spliced rope in which the uneven strands of two ragged ends have been carefully intermingled to give an invisible join. The 20th, while carrying on from the 19th, shows an upsurge of life in the whole community. The Yorkshire Dales Railway from Skipton, opened in 1902, was both a cause and a result of this. It enabled businessmen to travel daily to and from Bradford, it encouraged young people to go to Skipton schools and later to train for different kinds of work. It brought visitors in increasing numbers. The population diagram (Fig. 6) shows the beginning of what was to be a steady rise in population, leading to a need for more housing. Already many derelict cottages were being restored and modernised, and a new housing estate grew along the Hebden road, while larger houses were built elsewhere. No new industries had started in Grassington but employment increased in various ways in connection with visitors and new residents, and the quarries across the river were growing. In fact employment was steadily snowballing.

Grassington and Threshfield station was so-called because the line terminated midway between the two villages. This avoided the necessity of an expensive crossing of the Wharfe into Grassington itself, and also reflected hopes of the promoters to extend the railway up Wharfedale to Kettlewell and beyond. Such schemes had been floated since the 1840s, when the valley came close to economic and scenic transformation as a result of Parliament authorising a main line from Liverpool to Newcastle via Skipton, Grassington and Bishopdale that was almost built. Despite further attempts in the first decade of the century, some of which attracted opposition from what we now call preservationists, the railway never got beyond Grassington. The growth of motor transport, both buses and private cars, gave the line only a short life. In 1930 the passenger trains were withdrawn except for occasional excursions, and the portion of the branch from Swinden Quarry to Grassington closed down entirely in 1969. In more recent years, further competition from private cars has led to still more reduction of bus services.

In 1954 Grassington was included in the newly designated Yorkshire Dales National Park. The Yorkshire Dales is one of ten National Parks in England and Wales, and covers some 700 square miles of the finest countryside of the Central Pennines. The purpose of a National Park, which is largely financed by funds from central

Government, is to protect the natural beauty of the region. This includes the prevention of unsuitable and unsightly development in villages like Grassington, and measures to help the area cope with the ever increasing number of visitors from overseas as well as all parts of Britain who are inevitably attracted to our finest countryside. Grassington is now a Conservation Area and, as a natural focal point for the local tourist industry (now an important source of employment), it is fitting that a National Park administrative office should be situated in the village, dealing with local planning and related matters, the Park's warden and information services, public footpaths and bridleways and public transport services, as well as having a small Information Centre to help visitors to Grassington to enjoy their stay in the area.

The Grassington which has been described in the foregoing pages had its ups and downs. The population diagram showed the end of the great depression of the last decades of the 19th century and the beginning of recovery after 1901. Now in the final quarter of the 20th century the total has again reached the previous record of 1851.

If any ghosts from the mid 19th century walk in the Square and the by-paths of the village, they will see great differences, but they can still feel at home in many of the nooks and corners, and the overall pattern has changed very little. The people of today who want to know just where Wesley preached, where Grassington theatre was, where the nearest lead mines were and so on, cannot do better than take as guide Edward Gower's small booklet on Grassington (a Dalesman publication). In addition much light on the past is shed by the exhibits of the Upper Wharfedale Museum, which has been rehoused in the Square.

As for the future, that must be left to posterity, when the things of today have, in their turn, become history.

History Repeats Itself

One day in August 1745, 22 Grassington men carried out the traditional annual perambulation of the township boundary, or beating the bounds as it was generally called. Only eleven walked the whole way, the others going probably on horseback to join the walk at Priest Tarn on the far moor. Almost certainly there would be some boys also.

On May 14th 1977 a party of men, women and boys, 26 in all, did the complete walk on foot.

These are the only records of what was one of the oldest village ceremonies. Originally it had two purposes. It incorporated the Rogationtide blessing of the fields and the crops just before Whit-week, but that aspect did not survive the Reformation. More important historically its aim was to ensure that exact knowledge of the township boundary was passed on from generation to generation in the days before maps were made. For this reason boys were always included in the party and, according to tradition in many places, they were given a ceremonial beating at strategic points as an aid to memory!

The 1977 party of course had good maps, but 1745 was a few years too early for the Ordnance Survey. Perhaps some of the young men on that year's walk took the first surveyors round. Even with maps the boundary marks along the far end of the moor are not very clear, being rather worn down earth mounds, with no wall or fence.

This 1977 walk was done simply for the enjoyment and the sense of history being repeated, in part at least, but it is hoped that it will again be repeated, if not annually, at least before the boys of the 1977 perambulation get too old to lead the party!

A Miscellany of Dates

'L'il Emily's Bridge':

1814 First built mainly of wood by Jonathan Verity of Grassington for the owners of the mill. A private bridge, closed one day a year.

1860 Second, also mainly wood, built by Thomas Verity, grandson of the above. Still private.

1903 Bridge taken over by the Rural District Council and made public.

1904 Third, built of steel for the Council by a Glasgow engineering company.

* * *

1846 At this time and much earlier the Grassington Overseers of the Poor owned a blacksmith's shop (the present library) and the adjoining cottages, the rents of which went to keep the Poor Rate down, also six other cottages nearby let as a Poor House, but now demolished.

1857 An infants' school was held in the Independent Chapel.

1891 The first telegram reached Grassington, sent from Bolton to the Mechanics Institute with greetings from Bailey Harker.

1896 The Grassington Cricket Club was flourishing.

1906 The last spring fair for horned cattle was held.

1907 A telephone exchange was opened above the building where Garrs Lane and Gill Fold meet in the Square.

1909-11 Electricity and sewerage schemes now in operation.

1919 Grassington Hospital opened as a Sanatorium.

1921 The first houses of the new estate off Hebden road were built.

1955 Grass Wood was sold by the Duke of Devonshire to a timber merchant, later taken over by the Forestry Commission and in part by the Yorkshire Naturalists' Trust.

1957 The bus station opened.

1964-5 Main street lost its cobbles.

1970 onwards. Colvend developed as a Yorkshire Dales National Park centre.

Bibliography

The following books give supplementary information about Grassington:

Old Yorkshire Dales. Arthur Raistrick.

Pennine Walls. Arthur Raistrick.

Lead mining in the Yorkshire Dales. Arthur Raistrick.

Mines and T'Miners. J. M. Dickinson.

Upper Wharfedale. Harry Speight (1900)